Antique Cigar Cutters & Lighters

-Jerry Terranova
-Douglas Congdon-Martin

Schiffer Publishing Ltd
77 Lower Valley Road, Atglen, PA 19310

Library of Congress Cataloging-in-Publication Data

Terranova, Jerry.
Antique cigar cutters & lighters / Jerry Terranova & Douglas Congdon-Martin.
p. cm. -- (A Schiffer book for collectors)
Includes bibliographical references and index.
ISBN 0-88740-941-5 (hard)
1. Cigar lighters--Collectors and collecting. 2. Smoking paraphernalia--Collectors and collecting. I. Congdon-Martin, Douglas. II. Title. III. Series.
TS2280.T47 1996
688'.4--dc20 95-51110
CIP

Printed in China

ISBN: 0-88740-941-5

Published by Schiffer Publishing Ltd.
77 Lower Valley Road
Atglen, PA 19310
Please write for a free catalog.
This book may be purchased from the publisher.
Please include $2.95 for shipping.
Try your bookstore first.

We are interested in hearing from authors
with book ideas on related subjects.

To Doug's grandfather, William H. Leeks,
who loved his cigars to the end of his long life.

To Jerry's children who put up with missing him
on birthdays and holidays due his incessant hunt.

Acknowledgments

We thank Bill Bertoia, a friend of collectors everywhere, who introduced us to each other, giving birth to this volume.

Jerry thanks an old friend who started him on this addiction and all the antique dealers who have helped him build this collection.

At Schiffer Publishing we thank Dawn Stoltzfus, who recorded information during the photo shoot, and Mark S. Balbach for his wonderful design.

Contents

Introduction

The origins of the cigar are lost in prehistory. All we really know is that the use of tobacco was a widespread custom among the natives of the Americas long before the Europeans began their explorations. They cultivated the plant and used it for a variety of reasons and in a variety of forms. It was used as a medicinal plant, treating common illnesses of body and mind. It was a sacred herb, its gentle narcotic effect opening the smoker to the presence of the holy in tribal rituals. And it was used as it is today, as a recreational activity, bringing great pleasure to the imbiber.

Its introduction to the Europeans came very early. According to journals of the Columbus voyage, two members of his crew saw natives of San Salvador inhaling smoke from what they called "firebrands." The date was November 6, 1492, which can act as a milestone for the introduction of the cigar to the larger world. Columbus returned to Spain with his discovery.

In his wonderful study, *The Economic Development of the Cigar Industry in the United States*, Willis N. Baer cites the journals of Girolamo Benzoni of Milan, *Travels in America, 1541-1556.* Benzoni was an early observer of the New World, traveling here nearly eighty years before the earliest English settlements. Among the curiosities he found was the use of cigars. He writes:

> In this island (Canary Islands) as also in other provinces of these new countries, there are some bushes, not very large, like reeds, that produce a leaf in shape like that of a walnut, though rather larger, which is held in great esteem by the natives....When these leaves are in season, they pick them, tie them up in bundles, and suspend them near their fire place till they are very dry; and when they wish to use them, they take a leaf of grain (maize) and putting one of the others into it, they roll them round tight together; then they set fire to one end, and putting the other end into the mouth, they draw their breath up through it, wherefore the smoke goes into the mouth, the throat, the head, and they retain it as long as they can, for they find a pleasure in it, and so much do they fill themselves with this cruel smoke that they lose their reason.

While he may argue with the description of cigar smoke as "cruel," the cigar aficionado of today will recognize the power of the cigar.

Though the invention of the cigar is American, its early popularity was in Europe. Spain was at the heart of it, developing both the early market and the art of cigar making. The tobacco was grown in the West Indies, and by 1698 Spain had a monoply on cigar making in Cuba. The cigar industry in Cuba was the first. Its reputation as the source of the finest smokes began in these early years and has grown into a legend that continues today.

From Spain the use of cigars spread throughout the European continent. Around 1750 cigars became quite prevalent in England, though, according to Baer, their use was limited to the aristocratic classes.

In the American colonies, other forms of tobacco were much more popular than the cigar. While tobacco was an important cash crop for the early settlers, its manufacture was severely limited by the mother country. Those cigars that reached the colonists came by a circuitous route, from the West Indies to Spain to England and back to America.

Nevertheless a fledgling production of cigars began in the middle eighteenth century. Direct trade connections with the West Indies led to the importing, in limited quantities, of both cigars and cigar leaf. The leaf was combined with domestic tobacco to make cigars.

Meanwhile domestic leaf was developed which could stand on its own, particularly that of the Connecticut River Valley. According to Baer the domestic cigars were made by women, often as part of their household duties. The early production was centered around the families of the tobacco growers.

These local cigars did not measure up to the quality of the imported product, and in marketing them a clear distinction between them was made. What the American-made cigars lacked in quality they made up for in price, selling for about two for a penny.

While tobacco growing and manufacture was to be found through many of the colonies, the only noteworthy area of cigar manufacture in the colonial and early federal periods was in Pennsylvania. Baer reports that in the 1810 census, Pennsylvania was the only state mentioned as a producer of cigars. 29,061,000 were American made (domestic tobaccos) and 3,898,999 were "Spanish Segars."

In the early decades of the nineteenth century most cigar tobacco was still imported from the West Indies. With the exception of the Connecticut River valley there was no leaf raised that was suitable for the cigars. As demand for cigars increased and the government began to impose tariffs on imports, the cultivation of tobacco began to change and spread. In Connecticut, where it had been grown in small plots on family farms, farmers began to farm tobacco as a distinct business (*Baer, page 37*).

At the same time the farming of cigar tobacco spread to Pennsylvania, Connecticut, Florida, Georgia, New York, Ohio, Maryland, Virginia, and Wisconsin. Blended with some imported tobaccos, these locally grown tobaccos were the source of the great American cigar industry.

In the years from 1810 to 1860 the production of cigars evolved from a cottage industry to a shop industry. The work became more specialized and more men entered the field. "Yankee Traders" were sent from the cigar factories of Connecticut, loaded with domestic cigars which they use as a basis of trade and commerce throughout New England, New York, and New Jersey. The cigar trade spread to Massachusetts, and by 1842 New England concentrated its tobacco industry almost exclusively on cigars, leaving the manufacture of chewing tobacco to its southern competitors. *(Baer, page 38)*

Despite its growth during the early nineteenth century, the cigar was still a relatively minor player in the American tobacco industry. This was to change following the Civil War, and the cigar was to become the most popular form of tobacco in the nation.

It is difficult to say with certainty why this was so. In part it had to do with the war itself. The images caught by Mathew Brady and other chroniclers of the war showed the great heros brandishing their cigars like great symbols of authority. Grant and Sherman undoubtedly influenced the popularity of the cigar, and, in the years following the war, the cigar became associated with "manlihood." The cigar was part of the ensemble of the well-dressed Victorian gentleman. They could be found on the lips of presidents and millionaires, as well as the factory worker and office manager.

This new demand for cigars led to an explosion in the industry. The number of people employed as cigar makers grew from about 4000 in 1860 to about 80,000 in 1900. (*Cooper, page* 2) Another report estimates that there were 70,000 registered cigar making establishments in 1905, with an estimated 30,000 additional unregistered establishments. (*Petrone*)

At the same time the productivity of the manufacturers grew with the introduction of the cigar mold by German immigrants following the Civil War. Though seen as a threat by the hand making cigar artisans, the mold and accompanying industrial advances made the growth possible. According to Baer, a cigar maker could produce about 200 cigars per day with the all hand method, while with the mold the same person could produce on average 400 cigars per day, effectively doubling the production. In addition, it required less skill, so that cigar makers who had needed a four to five year apprenticeship for hand work, now could be trained in about a year. The introduction of the mold also allowed the industry to spread. A mold could be purchased for less than thirty dollars, which encouraged tobacconists, farmers, and other entrepreneurs to produce their own brands, either for distribution or private sale.

By 1904 cigars owned 60 percent of the tobacco market. The cigar would continue to dominate the market until the cigarette overtook it in the years following World War I.

The Golden Age and the Rise of Cutters

The golden age of cigars, from 1860-1910, corresponds with a revolution in marketing. Prior to this time most products, from flour to tobacco, was sold generically. Packed in bulk and identified only with the stenciled name of the manufacturer, a product was measured out and repackaged by the retailer, according to the customers wishes.

With industrialization and the rise of standardization of quality and measurement was born the concept of brand names. And with brand names came an explosion of advertising. It was a creative time. Each company tried to draw attention to itself with a more eye-catching poster or packaging or premium. With the perfection of chromolithography the advertising took on rich color, produced by using as many as twenty different stones to add different inks.

The cigar industry produced some of the most vivid and beautiful examples of the advertising art. Distinctive and beautiful graphics were produced to decorate the cigar boxes that carried their products, as well as the bands that encircled each smoke. At the same time their posters filled the walls of the tobacconist, trying to persuade the customer to buy them.

Indeed, the tobacconist's shop was a collage of advertising, from the fancy window displays, to the riot of colorful posters, to the hundreds of cigar box labels, and, of course, to the countertop cutters and lighters.

The cigar lighter was always lit, inviting the smoker to light up right there in the shop, and perhaps spend some time exchanging news and gossip before going on his way. It was usually combined with a cutter of some ingenious mechanical design. The cutter was a neat, clean way of opening the end of a cigar to allow the smoke to flow smoothly. In the cigar making process, the wrapper is rolled spirally around the bunch beginning at the tuck, the end that is lighted. The flap or "flag" is glued over the head of the cigar to hold the wrapper in place. This is what the cutter removes.

Running on kerosene, the countertop lighter/cutter was always ready for the customer to clip the end off of his cigar and light up. As he did so he would see some fancy advertising in cast iron, pierced tin, or reverse painted glass, reinforcing his choice of brands or encouraging him to switch brands on his next purchase.

Advertising cutters and lighters came in a variety of style and designs, which you will see in the pages which follow. Even cutters that were identical mechanically and in their basic design would have distinctive advertising shields or marquees that would remind the smoker who has provided this complimentary service.

Several companies were involved in the manufacturer of cutters and lighters. Edward Miller & Company of Meriden, Connecticut was producing beautiful cigar lighters as early as 1881, though they showed no cutters. In their catalog of that year they wrote:

> "In presenting you with our Illustrated Catalogue of Lamps and Cigar lighters, we would call especial attention to the Variety, Superior Style, and Finish of our Goods. We were granted a Medal and Diploma at the United States Centennial Exhibition, Philadelphia, 1876, for 'Variety, Taste, and Good Finish, noticeable in the entire Exhibit,' and a Diploma at the Sydney Exhibition, 1880.
>
> "We are constantly adding new designs to our line, and shall have at all times a line to select from that will fully meet the wants of the trade. We

solicit a portion of our orders."

By far the largest and earliest manufacturers of cutters included Brunhoff Manufacturing Co., of Cincinnati, and Erie Special Co., of Buffalo. Both arose at about the same time and produced a variety of cutters.

Erie Specialty Co. was founded in the late 1880s by E. Walker and Z.T. Brindley. Because the cutters bear Walker's name, we assume that he was the inventor of the partnership. Their patent for an Automatic Cigar Cutter is dated February 19, 1889, which, they claimed in their 1897 catalog, was the earliest. Other cutter patents are dated 1891 and 1895. Every cutter they manufactured was available plain or with custom advertisements, embossed on metal plates. Lighters were also available, as were combination lighters and cutters.

From their 1897 catalog we learn that they moved into a new plant in 1896, thinking it "adequate to our wants for some time to come." They had so underestimated the demand for their product that, in 1897, they had to expand again, "to nearly double their former capacity. Other than these facts and the quality of their products, little is known of the Erie Specialty Company at this time.

Brunhoff Manufacturing Co. was founded in 1890, and grew to become one of the largest advertising and merchandizing display companies in the nation. Its specialty was in metal and glass advertising pieces, of which their line of cigar cutters is exemplar. The company continued to produce point-of-purchase advertising under the Brunhoff name until 1959 when it was sold to American Art Works, another early name in advertising, and a division of Rapid-American Corporation.

The demise of the countertop public cigar cutter may have come in 1913. The understanding of communicable disease was growing more and more sophisticated, and it was suspected that the spread of tuberculous and other infectious ailments had something to do with saliva. Because cigar smoker habitually licked the end of his cigar before using the cigar cutter, it was reasonable to assume that the cutters may contribute to the spread of these dread diseases. In 1913 the government issued a warning to smokers to stop using the community cigar cutters present in practically every tobacco shop in the country.

The use of the cutter at home, nevertheless, continued unabated. It is these that show the most creativity. They range from large desktop models to small cutters that fit in the vest pocket. They are found constructed of tin or cast as Vienna bronzes. The forms they take range from beautiful, three dimensional figures to simple scissors.

Whatever their form they have the same purpose: to enhance the quality of the smoke. Zino Davidoff, in *The Connoisseur's Book of the Cigar*, suggests that there are three methods of cutting a cigar, "by pinching with the fingers, using the teeth, or with the aid of an instrument." (*page 11 ff.*) The goal is a clean, small opening that allows an "appropriate amount" of smoke to be produced. He continues

> "Any method of cutting that respects these imperatives is admissible. American smokers, in general, use a cutter. Others - not the most sophisticated - chew off the end. Outside the fact that a very sharp cut is required (and this may call for two or three bites), this method does not permit much precision...I never practice or recommend such a method...
>
> "Despite the opinion of some, it is not shameful to use [a cigar cutter], especially if it has been well chosen. Ordinary cigar cutters, which make a round or beveled cut, are not to be condemned."

In contrast to Davidoff's less than an enthusiastic endorsement of cigar cutters, the Cigar Institute of America suggested that their use was to be preferred. In 1942 they published *The Story of Cigars*, a book for retailers of cigars, which shared with them the information and knowledge they needed to become informed salespeople. It contained a brief history of the cigar, information about its manufacture, and bits of information about the lore of cigars and the famous people who were aficionados of them. It also had tips to pass along to customers. "Your customers will naturally appreciate anything you can do to increase their smoking pleasure."

Among these tips was this:

> "Sticking a pin in the head of a cigar does not make it draw better. The best way to prepare a cigar for smoking is to clip off the end with a cigar cutter or to puncture it cleanly and not too deeply. After cutting the head, blow through from the tuck. This will remove any tobacco dust caused by cutting the head..."

With that official endorsement, it is possible to appreciate the beauty and ingenuity of these machines. That is the real point of this volume, and the objects here will fascinate the reader. They represent an era of invention and creativity that is unique in the history of the world. And they bespeak a love affair with the "firebrand" cigar that, despite the ebb and flow of fashion, is enduring from generation to generation.

In singing the praises of the cigar the author of *The Story of Cigars* wrote, "Long after many marvels of the present generation have been superseded by new inventions, civilized man will seek relaxation and tranquility of spirit through the enjoyment of a good cigar."

ORDER 55.

WALKER'S

Cigar Cutter.

OPERATED WITH ONE HAND.

REVOLVING KNIFE.

CUTS CLEAN.

BREAKS NO CIGARS.

SPRINGS DO NOT BREAK.

This cutter can be had PLAIN, or with an ADVERTISEMENT printed on front end of wood base, extended two inches, in lots of three dozen or more.

THIS CUTTER GIVES PERFECT SATISFACTION.

Prices Quoted on Application, According to Quantity.

ORDER 56.

WALKER'S

CIGAR CUTTER.

With a very attractive embossed advertising plate on top, at proper angle, to attract attention of the smoker.

We enamel around name of cigar, making the brand VERY PROMINENT.

IT REQUIRES BUT ONE HAND TO OPERATE THIS CUTTER.

THESE ELEGANT DESIGNED PLATES FURNISHED ONLY IN GROSS AND LARGER LOTS.

Prices Quoted on Application, According to Quantity.

ORDER 54.

WALKER'S

CIGAR CUTTER.

Patented May 19, 1891.

THIS IS THE MOST POPULAR ADVERTISING CIGAR CUTTER EVER PUT ON THE MARKET.

The embossed plates used on them are the finest produced for the purpose, being very artistic and attractive. As a permanent advertisement it is unequalled, as it is constantly being used by the smoker.

ON ORDER FOR A GROSS OR MORE, WE FURNISH A

SPECIAL DESIGNED PLATE.

We have made several improvements in our plates, which make the advertisement very attractive.

Prices Quoted According to Quantity.

ORDER 57.

WALKER'S

Cigar Cutter

AND

Revolving Advertisement.

Patented August 21, 1895.

AS AN advertising device for cigars, this cutter surpasses all competitors.

The CIRCULAR ADVERTISING DISK IS INSTANTLY REVERSED when the smoker cuts tip of cigar, which attracts so much attention that the operation is repeated until the cigars advertised are indelibly impressed in memory.

The Advertising Cards used are ARTISTICALLY DESIGNED, making them attractive to the eye.

NEW IMPROVEMENTS TO THIS CUTTER.

VERY STRONG AND DURABLE.

PRICES IN GROSS AND LARGER LOTS QUOTED ON APPLICATION.

ORDER 58.

WALKER'S

CIGAR CUTTER.

A NEW DESIGN, VERY CATCHY.
ORNAMENTAL BASE.
FINE EMBOSSED METAL PLATE.
EASY TO OPERATE.

CAN BE COMBINED WITH A LIGHTER.

PRICES ON APPLICATION IN GROSS AND LARGER LOTS.

ORDER 59.

Patented Feb. 19, 1889. Other patents to be applied for.

(SEE NOTICE, PAGE 21.)

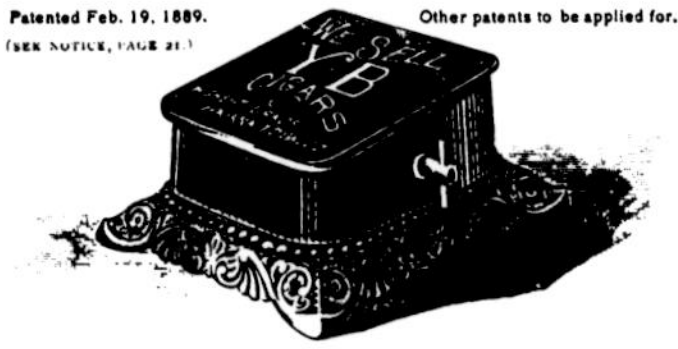

WALKER'S

Automatic Cigar Cutter.

- NEW DESIGN.
- JUST OUT.
- ALL NICKEL.
- ARTISTICALLY DESIGNED PLATES.
- ENAMELED ANY COLOR DESIRED.
- ALWAYS READY.
- KNIVES HAVE A SHEARING CUT.

OWING to the pressure being above cutting point and evenly distributed around the end, and the point not coming in contact with anything, it prevents all possibility of breaking the cigar.

WE FURNISH ANY SPECIAL DESIGNED PLATE DESIRED IN GROSS LOTS AND UPWARD.

Price single cutter plain plate $2.50

ORDER 60.

Patented Feb. 19, 1889. Other patents to be applied for.

(SEE NOTICE, PAGE 21.)

WALKER'S

Automatic Cigar Cutter.

ALL NICKEL.
ENAMEL EMBOSSED PLATES.
MADE IN ANY DESIGN.
WILL NOT BREAK CIGARS.
UNEQUALLED AS AN ATTRACTIVE ADVERTISEMENT.
OPERATED SAME AS ORDER 59.

SPECIAL DESIGNED PLATES MADE IN GROSS LOTS AND UPWARD.

Price single cutter, plain plate $2.00

ORDER 65.

Patented Aug. 21, and Feb. 26 1895.

Walker's Cigar Cutter with Revolving Advertisement.

NEW DESIGN. ALL NICKEL FINISH. ENAMELED EMBOSSED PLATES.

Space for Two Separate Advertisements on the Revolving Card.

EVERY CUT OF THE CIGAR REVOLVES THE PLATE AND DISPLAYS TWO SEPARATE ADVERTISEMENTS.

Owing to the large plate and revolving cards, more brands of cigars can be advertised on this cutter than any other made.

SPECIAL DESIGNED PLATES AND ENGRAVED CARDS FURNISHED ON GROSS ORDERS AND UPWARD.

Prices Quoted on Application According to Quantity.

ORDER 68.

WALKER'S

Cigar Cutter AND Lighter Combined.

LARGE POLISHED NICKEL LAMP.

Mounted on a finely finished hardwood base, with the celebrated WALKER No. 54 CIGAR CUTTER.

Special advertising plate in gross lots or upward, or plain nickel plate in less quantity.

Price $2.50

ORDER 70.

WALKER'S CIGAR LIGHTER.

LARGE LAMP, NICKELED.
FINELY CARVED METAL BASE, NICKELED.

Especially Designed for Advertising Purposes

ENGRAVED Card securely fastened in circular space makes an ATTRACTIVE ADVERTISEMENT.

Price $2.00

ORDER 72.

For Description of Cutter See Order 60.

ALL NICKEL FINISH.

Patented Feb. 19, 1889. Other Patents to be applied for.

(SEE NOTICE, PAGE 21.)

WALKER'S

Automatic Cutter and Lighter Combined.

Large Lamp, Will Hold Sufficient Oil to Burn Several Days.

Special designed plate furnished in gross lots and upwards.

Price, single one, plain plate $3.50.

ORDER 73.

ALL NICKELED.

Walker's Cigar Lighter and Cutter.

THE MOST POPULAR COMBINATION LIGHTER AND CUTTER EVER PUT ON THE MARKET.

ATTRACTIVE. DURABLE. USEFUL.

Lamp will hold sufficient oil to burn several days.

In gross lots, special enamel advertising plates. In small quantities, plain plates.

Price $2.50

ORDER 74.

NEW 1897 DESIGN.

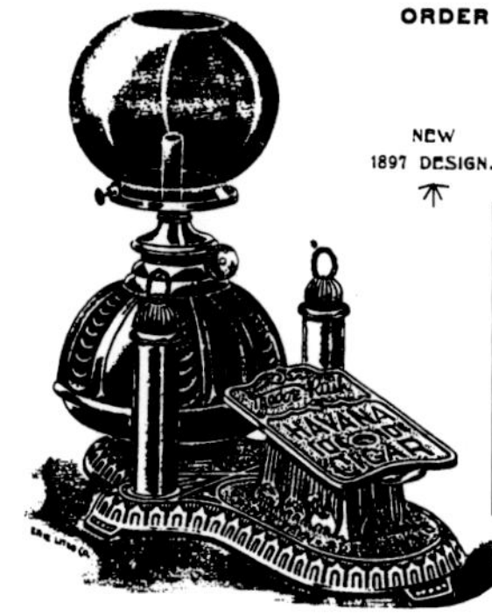

WALKER'S

Cigar Lighter and Cutter.

LARGE ADVERTISING PLATE.
SPACE FOR ADVERTISEMENT ON BASE.

ORNAMENTAL AND VERY ATTRACTIVE.

All parts nickeled. Made only in gross and larger lots.

Price $2.50

ORDER 69.

WALKER'S

Cigar Cutter and Lighter Combined.

COMBINATION LIGHTER AND CIGAR CUTTER

OPERATED WITH ONE HAND.

Advertisement printed on front end of wood base, when desired, in quantities to suit purchaser.

Price $2.50

ORDER 71.

WALKER'S CIGAR LIGHTER.

LAMP TUBE AND ALCOHOL SOCKET NICKELED.

FINELY CARVED NICKEL BASE.

Makes an Attractive, Durable Lighter.

Price $1.50

AT THE HOME
or
OFFICE

I

Figural Desk Cutters

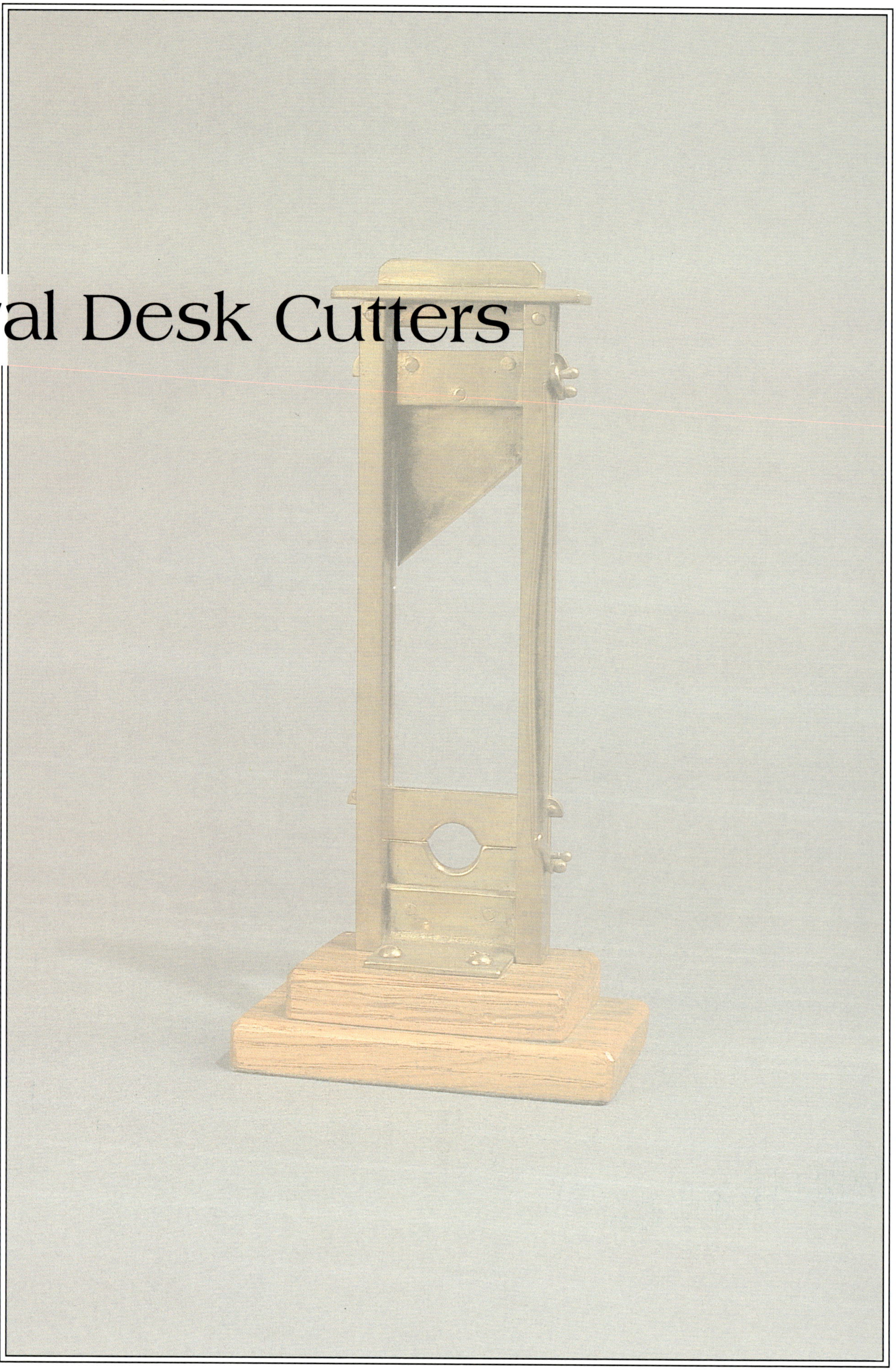

Seated man in a long coat with a fez. One hand holds a bottle and the other is pulled to cut a cigar placed in his mouth. 3.5" x 7.5".

This shouting peddler woman has her mouth open for a cigar. The arm holding the shoe is pulled to cut, while the basket hanging off other arm receives the cutting. 4" x 9".

The mouth of this marble-based bronze bust opens and closes to cut the cigar. 6" x 5".

Below: Vienna bronze polychrome black boy. The orange he is eating pulls out to reveal the cutter. 5" x 1.5".

Uniformed naval figure standing beside a castle tower cutter, which has a lever on the side to activate it. 7" x 9".

Above Right and Right: Military drummer of metal and brass. The hole for the cigar is in his back pack. When you push down his right arm to cut the cigar, the left arm raises the cymbal to reveal the tray for the tip. Striker on back. Marked "Mistersch." on bottom. 5" x 8".

A beautiful brass acrobat. He leans back to activate the cutters located in the vaulting horse. 3" x 5.5".

These gentlemen on their trunks would be glad to cut your cigar if you place it in the hole and push their heads down. White metal, 3.75" x 9".

This gentleman, called "The Butler," will cut a cigar at the turn of the head. Place the cigar in his hat and turn the head to activate. Brass, 4" x 8".

Right: These squatters have a cutter in their bellies. Pressing the head activates the blade, and the tip falls into the chamber pot behind. Among collectors this cutter is known as "man on potty." Brass, 3" x 6".

The Singing Man cigar cutter. Pull the arm down and he bites off the tip, which comes out the tail of his coat and falls into the stump. Metal, 6" x 7.5".

This wonderful variation of The Singing Man has an expanded base and a polychrome brick doorway behind. Cast iron, 8.5" x 12".

The lever activates the cutter located in this young man's mouth. Known as "The Dunce," it is metal on a wood base, 4.5" x 7.5".

Intricately designed chicken coop cutter, with four metal pieces mounted in a chicken yard scene on a wooden base. Overall dimensions, 8.5" x 7".

More variations of The Singing Man. Put the cigar in his mouth and pull down the book to cut your cigar. The one on the left has an opening in the back for the tips. The one on the right lets the tips fall underneath and has the markings "O.G. Hull, Kansas City, M." 6.25" x 8.5".

A view of the cigar cutter in the chicken coop.

Brass boy on sled. The cutter is at the front and the matchbox is at his back. 3" x 2.5".

A multipurpose cigar fixture, "The Monk" includes a cutter, a cigar holder, matchbox holder, and striking surface. There is also a slot so it can be used as a bank, allowing the smoker to save up for his next box of cigars. Wood base, metal top and castings. 7.5" x 9".

Humpty-Dumpty type cigar cutter. The arm is the lever. 2.5" x 2.5".

Two black iron butlers, identical shape, but the mouth of the one on the left opens to act as an ashtray and the one on the right is an kerosene lighter. The flame comes from the nose, and the reservoir is in the head. The cutter is on the tray he is holding, and there is a matchbox holder in the other hand. 6" x 11".

This musician is said to be a Dickens character. The cutter is activated when the leg is pushed down. Metal, 6.75" x 8".

Armored knight on a pedestal. The cutter is activated by pushing the knight down. On the side are four crests, one of which has the initials J.D. 3" x 7".

Above Left: Two brass German soldiers atop a wooden humidor box. The first is carrying a teapot that is an kerosene lighter, the wick coming from the pot with the flame in the spout. It has a cutter above the leg. The second carries a matchbox holder. The locked box opens to reveal a humidor drawer. On the front of the base is painted "Immer an der Wand lang," (Always on the long wall). 10" x 11".

Left: Cast iron pipe and matchbox holder, cigar cutter, and ashtray. L.V. Aronson 1922, Made in U.S.A. 10" x 4".

Desktop cigar cutters in the form of people. The two boys smoking are Tom Sawyer and Huck Finn. 6" to 7".

Brass tiered cutter, matchholder, and cigar rack. The figure looks as if it was meant to be holding something, probably a lighted match. 13" x 11.5".

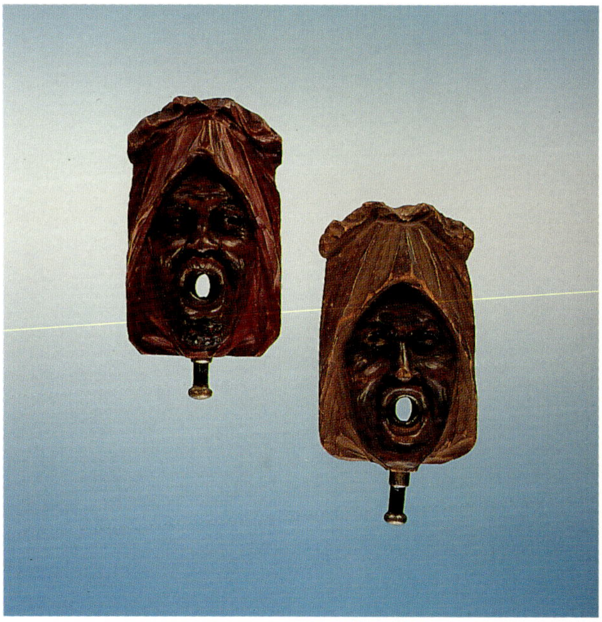

Carved wooden head cigar cutters. 4.5" to 1.5".

Desktop Beelzebubs. 5.25" to 5.75" in length.

Handheld brass cigar cutter with a figure of a young woman on the handle, 6" x 1".

Above Left and Left: Bronze American Indian bust which serves as a humidor, match and cigar holder. 16.5" x 15".

Nude women figural cigar cutters, bronze with marble base. Left: 8.25" x 3", right: 6.25" x 3".

Right and Above Right: Bronze with marble base cutter, the woman's legs open to cut the cigar, 8.25" x 2.5".

Similar to the earlier example, except that it has no color added. 8.25" x 2.5".

Bronze female figure in the style of the Vargas girls, on her back with marble base. The legs open to reveal the cigar cutter. 4" x 8.25".

These shapely legs make attractive desktop cutters. The cutter is behind the garter. The middle leg was silvertoned. 5" x 1.5".

Bronze dancer sitting on marble base. The skirt lifts to reveal the cigar cutter. Signed C. Kaab. 3.25" x 6.75".

These lounging women are just waiting to cut a cigar. Handheld brass cutters. Left: 5.25" x 1". Middle: 6" x 2". Right: 9" x 3".

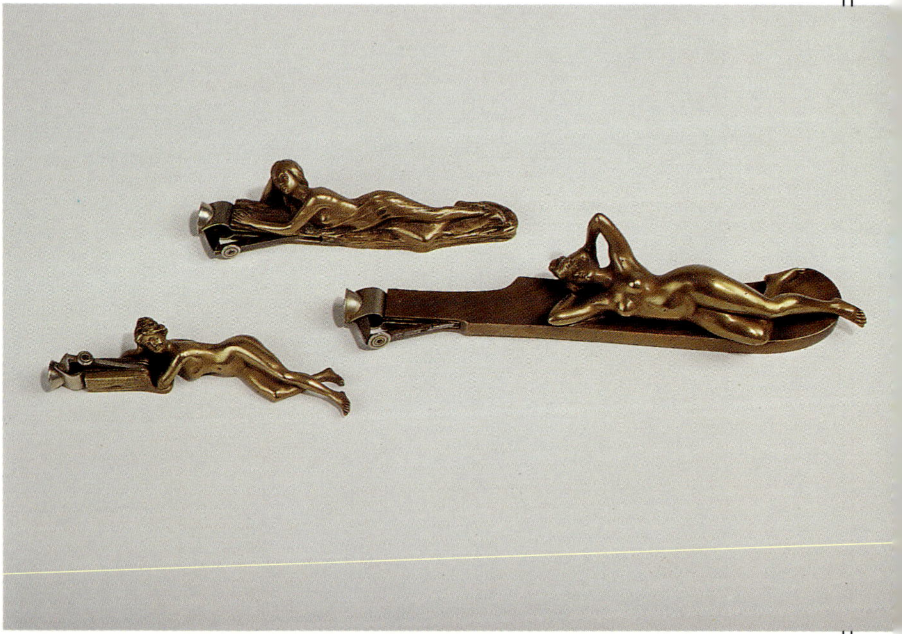

An imitation of the previous cutters; brass plated white metal on marble, 9" x 3".

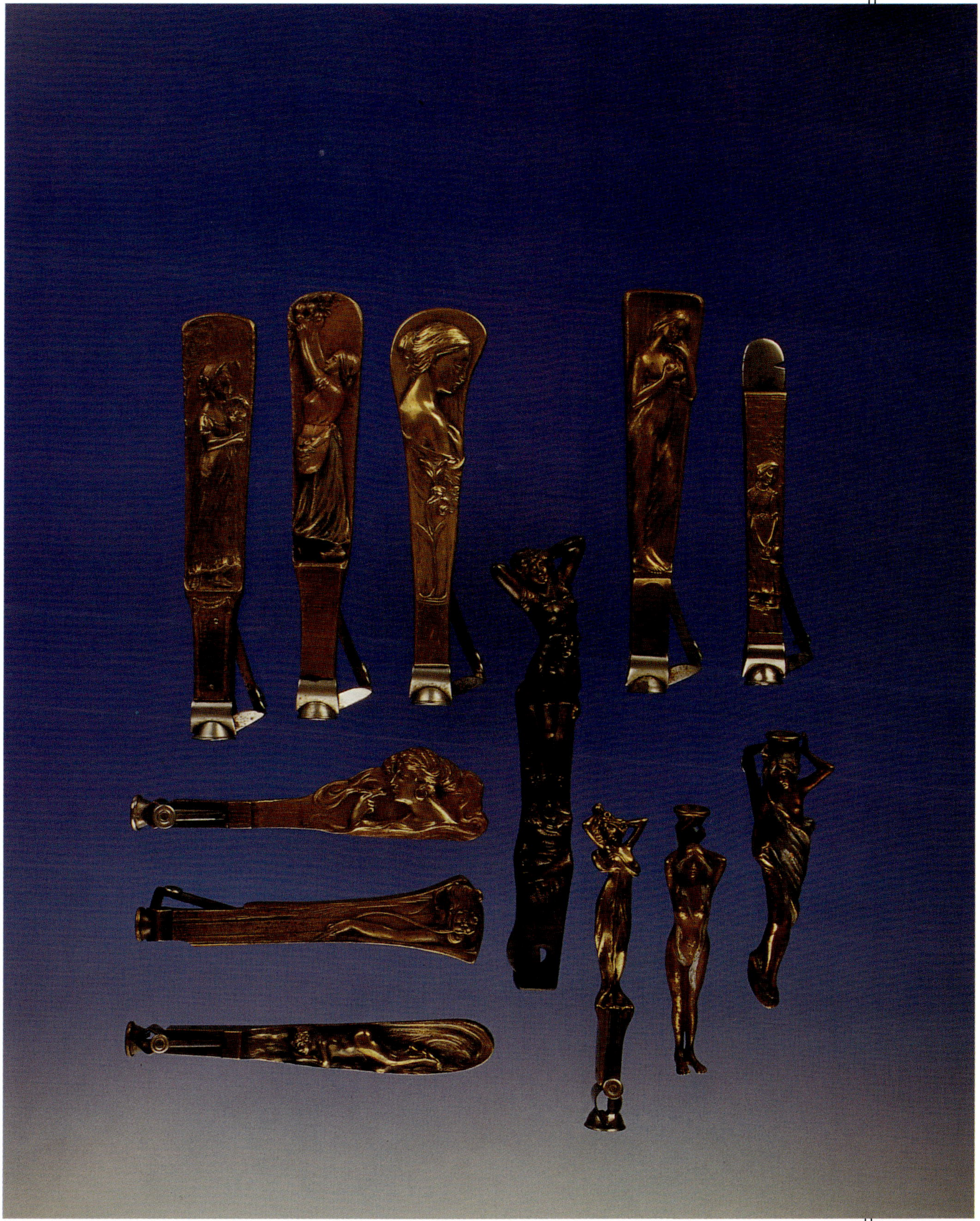

These handheld desktop cutters feature a variety of female figures. The painted cutters are Austrian bronze. 8" to 4.5".

Farm Animals

These three donkeys are cutters and games. You insert ball bearing into the pack, and either the ears wiggle or the tail moves for heads or tails. The one on the far right has a 49 on its saddle, for the 49ers, and has three cutter holes. 5" x 9"

A ram jumping a fence is the handle of this wonderful cutter. When the ram is pushed back to cut the cigar, a pin in its tail picks up a match from the reservoir underneath. Brass on a wood base. 5" x 4".

Small bull-shaped cutter. His tail lifts to cut the cigar through the hole in its flank. 3" x 1.5".

A handcarved bull adorns the back of this wooden desk set. It includes a cigar holder, matchholder, and a brass cutter on a handpainted porcelain dish. 13" x 10".

A brass horse cutter with foliage. 6.5" x 1.5".

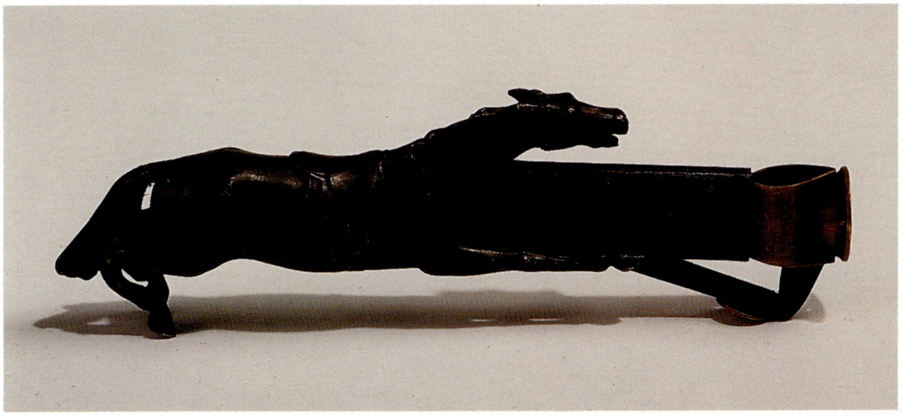

This handheld desktop cutter features a horse jumping a fence. Metal, 5" x 1.5".

Desktop brass, sterling silver, and bronze horse cutters.

Metal horse cigar cutter, lever-activated by pulling down the tail. 8.5" x 7.25".

Brass pig cutter. Pull down the tail to cut the cigar. 5" x 4".

Brass-toned pigs with the cutting mechanism in the tail. Left: 7" x 4.5", right: 6" x 4".

Copper-toned pig cigar cutter on base. Cast iron, 7" x 5".

Polychrome pig cutter.

This pig works like most of the others: the tail pulls down to act as the cigar cutter. There is, however, a hole under stomach to catch the tip. The slop bucket is an nice additional touch. 7.5" x 3.5".

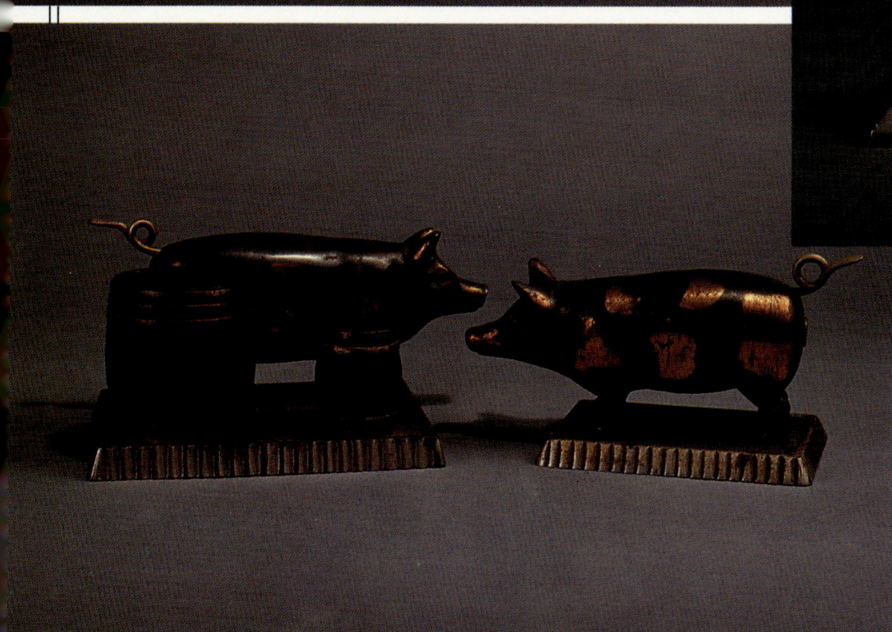

Japanned pig cigar cutter.

Wild Animals &Birds

Bronze ashtray and cutter. The cutter is in the bear's mouth. 5.25" x 3".

This menacing coiled snake has jaws that open and close to cut the cigar with its fangs. Brass, 3" x 4".

Brass and copper cutter, with serpent. 4" x 6.5", mark and 76 on bottom.

Brass cutters. On the left is a kangaroo with an ashtray, 5.5" x 5". On the right is a fox, 7" x 7.5".

The brass fox cutter sits across the bowl of this ashtray and matchholder. 8" x 7.5".

This crouching fox is ready for action. The cutter has small hollow below it to catch the tips. 10" x 3.5".

This nicely carved wolf in girl's clothing, appears to be on the way to Grandmother's house. It stands atop a cigar rack and has a matchsafe on its back. The rack and carving rotates on the base. Wood, 7" x 11".

Handheld desk top cutter in the form of a roaring tiger with jungle foliage. Brass, 7" x 2".

Brass lion on marble base, with a cutter in its mouth. 4" x 3".

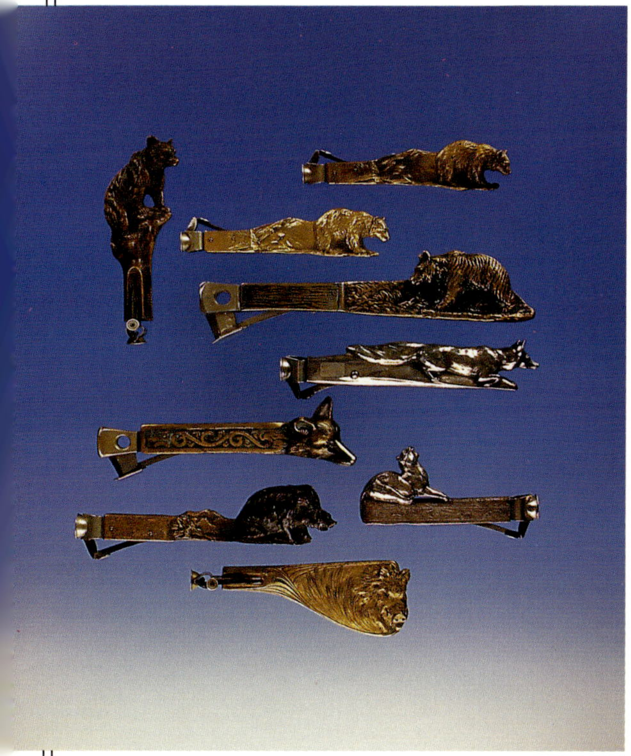

Desktop brass, sterling silver, and bronze wildlife cutters. Their lengths are from 8.5" to 6".

This giraffe cutter is on an ashtray with a matchbox holder. The cutter is at the base of the neck, and the tip falls out of the back. Marked Goberg Ges. Gesch. on bottom. 9" x 11".

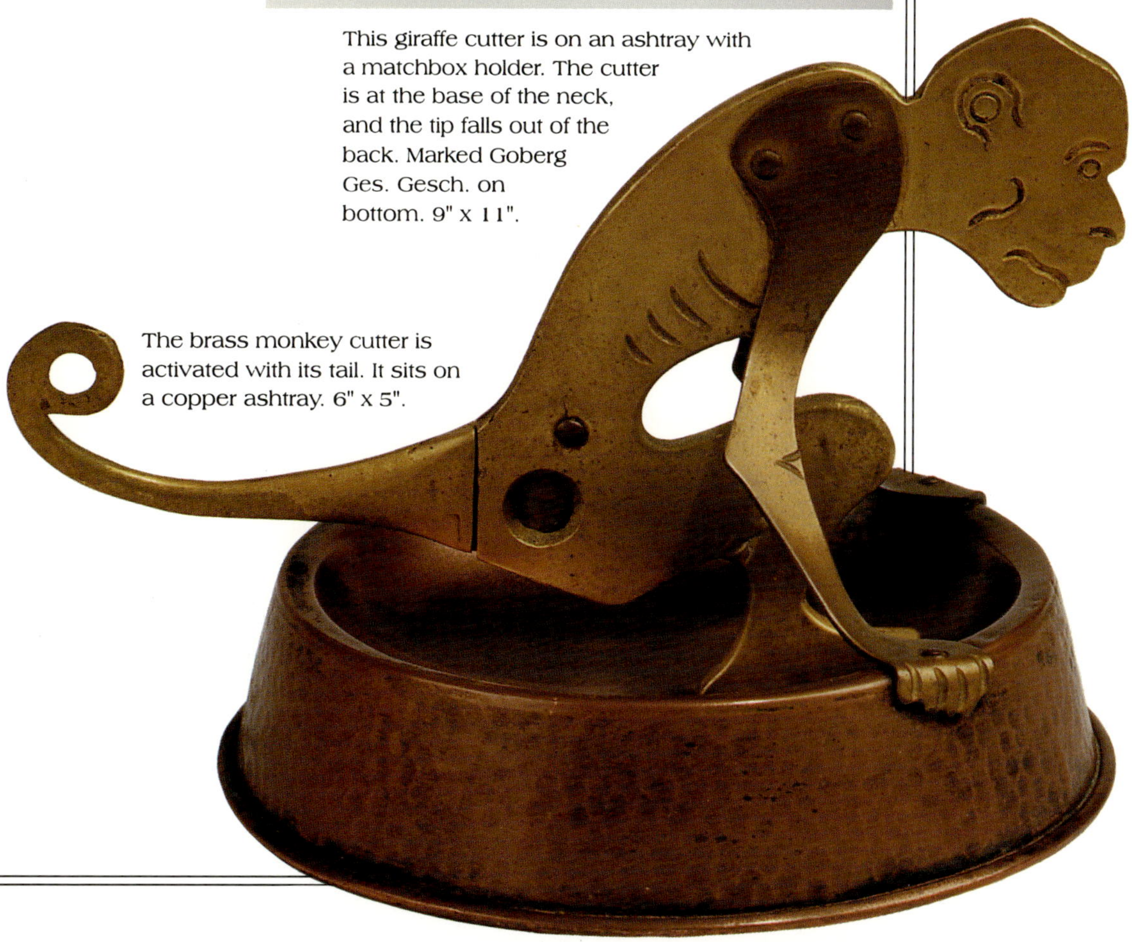

The brass monkey cutter is activated with its tail. It sits on a copper ashtray. 6" x 5".

Left: Solid brass bulldog standing, with a cigar cutter in its arms. 2" x 4.5". Right: Standing elephant holding a cigar cutter. Solid brass with Bakelite or ivory tusks. 6.5" x 3".

Cast iron elephant cigar cutter. The trunk is pulled to activate the cutter on its back, and the tip is expelled out the back. 7.5" x 6".

A wonderful circus elephant cutter reminiscent of Jumbo. Metal, 5.5" x 6".

Humidor, cutter, and striker lighter. Wood and silverplate, with brass lining the humidor, 6.25" x 6.25".

These elephants are combination cutters and lighters. The trunk acts as a lever to activate the cutter in the top of the head. Cast iron, 11.5" x 7" without base or burner.

Desktop brass and bronze elephants. The tusks could be ivory. 8" to 5.25".

Deeply sculpted brass stag head cutter with foliage. 7" x 2".

A seal graces this sterling silver and tortoise shell cutter. Three holes. The bottom has a tag which reads: "Sterling and Tortoise, Cigar Cutter, London, 1890, OYN 2144." Hallmark HA on side. 5" x 3.5".

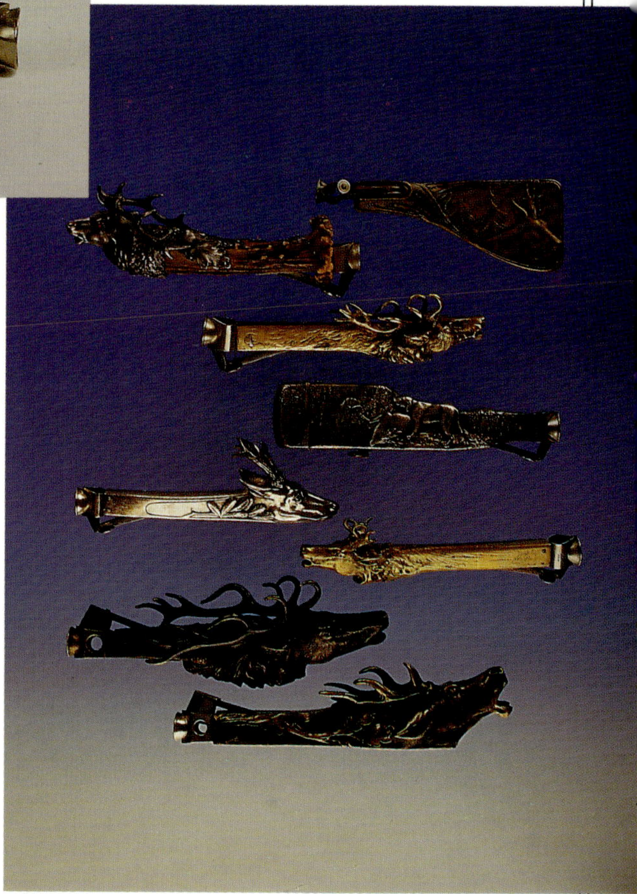

Desktop brass,sterling silver and bronze stag deer and elk. The handle of the upper left cutter is antler. 7" to 5.5" length.

Brass frog cutter with pullout cutter in its mouth. 2" x 1.5".

Brass turtle cutter with two hole sizes on shell. The head pushes down to cut the cigar. On the bottom there is a trap door to empty the tips, and the markings Gesetzlich Geschlützt, Eisenwerk Lauchhammer, 2750. 5.5" x 2.5".

Polychrome bronze lizard with pullout cutter. 6" x 2".

Desktop brass, sterling silver and bronze fish and crocodiles. All 6".

This crocodile (alligator?) has the cutter in its mouth, the lever emerging from the top of the snout. 6.25" x 1".

This beautiful brass and copper grasshopper cutter, is activated by the antennae, with the tip falling into the bowl. 6.5" x 4.5".

Brass cigar cutter on an ornate stand, with a decorative eagle on a ball. Large ornate Q on the cutter, 2969 B on base. 6.5" x 4".

A handsome brass owl-face cigar cutter and ashtray with cigar rest. The beak opens and closes to activate the cutter. 6.5" x 6.5".

This brass cutter takes the form of a long-beaked bird. The tip falls into the copper bowl ashtray. 4" x 5".

Below: Bird cutters and ashtrays. The cutters are activated by moving the beak or tail. The two on the left are similar, brass and copper, 4.5" x 6 and 6" x 6". The third one has Schutz on bottom, 6" x 6.5", and the one on the right is a parrot, 8" x 7".

Metal bird with cutter in the tail. 6" x 7".

Metal bird cutters. Left to right: bronze with copper bowl, 4.5" x 6"; copper bowl with cast iron figure; copper bowl with cast iron figure, 5" x 9"; brass with metal bowl, 4.5" x 6". The cutters are in the beaks.

This parrot on a stand is a cigar cutter, candleholder, and matchbox holder. The cutter is in the shoulder. 5" x 9".

Penguin cutter with matchbox holder. The cutter is under the beak. Marked Goberg Ges. Gesch. on bottom. Metal, 7" x 9".

Parrot cigar cutter. Pull the top feather back and beak opens and shuts to cut the cigar.

Pelican cigar cutter. Pull back the top feathers to cut, the tips fall into the beak which lifts up to empty. Metal, 4" x 7.5".

Pair of crow-shaped cigar cutters whose beaks do the cutting when you push their tail feathers down. 9.5" x 4".

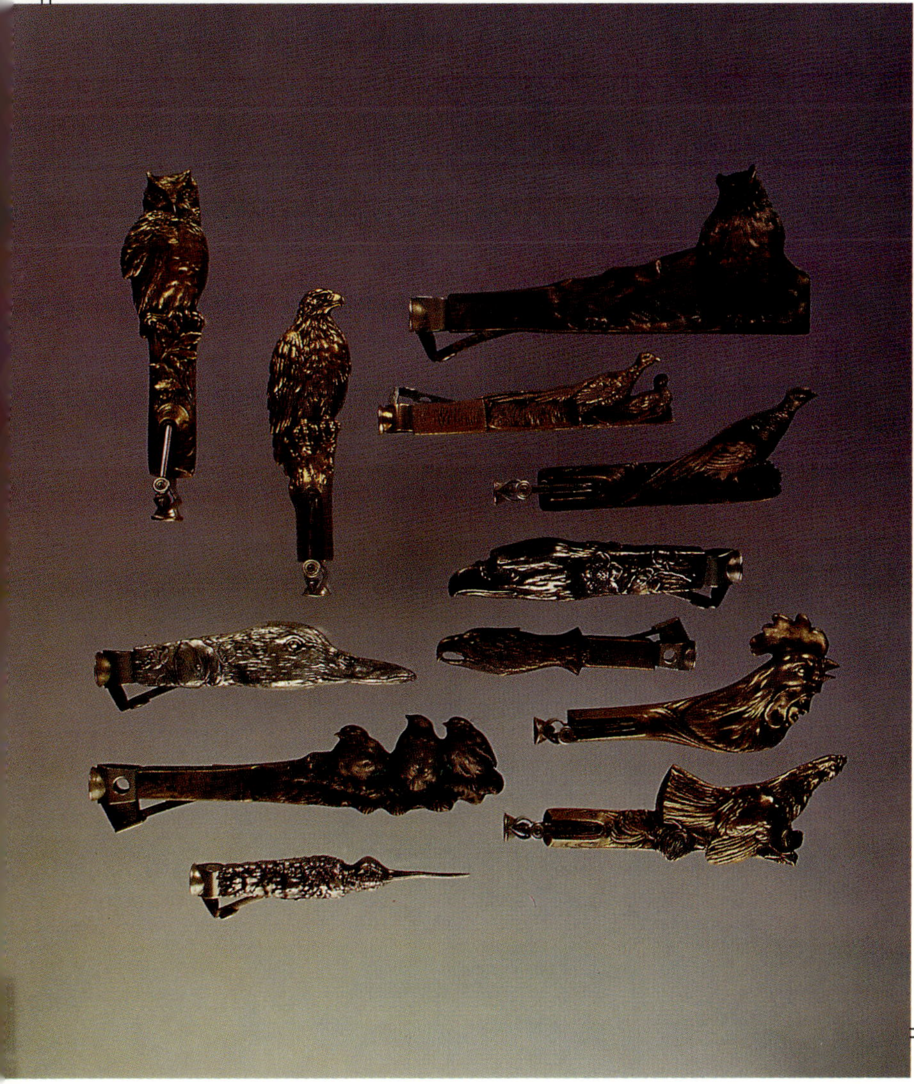

Brass, sterling silver, and bronze handheld cigar cutters, average length about 6.5". Note: the rooster is not actually a bird. If you look close, you will see a face. This is a Native American wearing a rooster headdress.

This chicken cutter has a rather surprised look about it. Perhaps it has to do with the cutter behind its tail. 2" x 1".

Dogs & Cats

Right: Brass doghouse cutter on a Bakelite base. The chimney is pushed to cut, and the doghouse flips open to clean. It is marked MS inside. 2.5" x 2".

This black cat cutter and ashtray are cast iron. The tail is the lever to activate the cutter. 5" x 7".

Right: A bulldog stands watch on this brass desk set. It includes a cutter, matchbox holder, and cigar lighter. Marked K on bottom. 3.75" x 3.5".

Nicely sculpted brass collie sitting on boards. The dog pivots to activate the cutter in the boards. Marked Ges. Geschutz Austria on bottom. 6" x 2.5".

The bull dog watches over the push-down cigar cutter and matchbook holder. The brass fixture is mounted on a wood base. 10" x 4".

Right: Put your cigar in the mouth of this dog in the barrel and push the dog down. It cuts the cigar and the tip falls out the bottom. Metal, marked Kusch'dich!

A rakishly dressed bronze dog in a wooden barrel. The top hat is trimmed in velvet to allow it to be compressed and stretched to operate the cutter in his mouth. There is a plug on a chain in back of barrel, which pulls out to empty tips. English, 6" x 9".

A standing mastiff. The mouth takes the cigar. It is cut when his paw is shaken, and the tip falls into a hole on the bottom. There are striking surfaces on the sides. Polychrome cast iron, 4" x 9".

Right: "Hunting" dog takes on a new meaning with this gun-toting cutter dressed in hunter's garb. The cutter is under the tail, which acts as the lever. Metal, 5.5" x 9".

Below: Three dachshunds cutters, with the cutters under the tail. Left: Cast iron, cigar in mouth, 9" x 4". Middle: Brass on wood base, 11" x 5". Right: Similar to one on left, but holding a hat,11.5" x 4".

This unusually shaped dachshund is a cutter and candleholder, and has a hat which is a matchsafe. Cast iron, 13" x 10".

Brass dog holding copper kettle, with matchbox and ashtray. The neck is pulled up to cut the cigar. 6.5" x 9".

Two dachshund cutters with matchbox holders. The cutter is operated by lifting and lowering the tail. Left: cast iron; right: brass. 8" x 3" x 3.5".

Identical barking dogs show the pullout cutters at rest and in their action position. Brass, 2" x 2.5"

Two bulldog cigar cutters, with pullout cutters in their mouths. Left: polychrome, 3" x 2". Right: 2.5" x 2".

This poodle desk piece has the cigar cutter hole in its back, with the tail as the lever. D.R.G. Musterschutz on bottom. 7" x 5.5".

Small brass handheld cutter, with dog head and leaves at one end and cutter at the other, with hallmark. 3" x 1".

This dog's head handheld cutter has a brass finish. On the cutter is a Sellenger, Germany hallmark consisting of a circle with arrows. Sellenger made only the mechanisms for the cutters. 5.5" x 1.5".

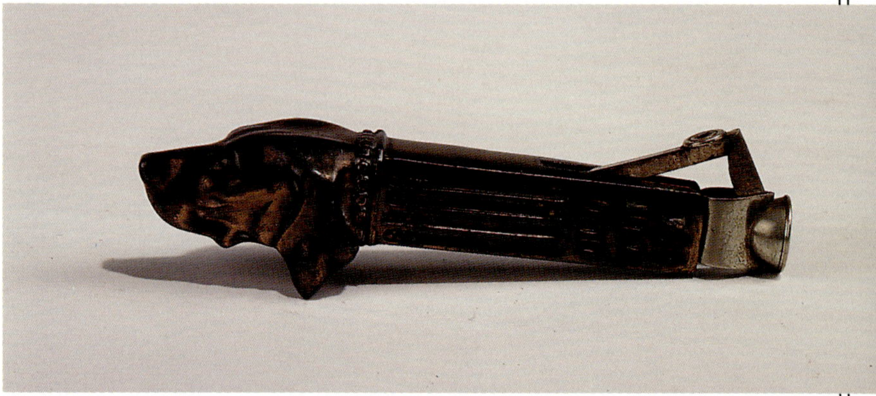

Brass handheld cutter with three dimensional sculpted dog's head and decorative foliage. 5.5" x 1".

Dog-shaped handheld cigar cutters in brass, sterling silver, and bronze.

Architectural

Metal cigar cutter in the form of a stone fort. The window/hole in the front is the cutter activated by pulling down the lever on the side. 3.75" x 4".

The Eiffel Tower has a cutter at the top, activated by pushing down on the peak. There is a pullout drawer that is a matchsafe. 3" x 8".

A brass Sphinx and its pedestal sit on a wooden base. The cutter is in the pedestal and there is a slide-out door in front for emptying the tips. 3.75" x 5".

Pewter Eiffel Tower cutter on painted wooden base. The top of tower is pushed down to activate cutter. 3" x 5".

Wood and brass desk set with cutter, matchholders, and a hand painted humidor with a cigar rack in the lid. 8.5" x 7".

Rosewood and ivory architectural desktop humidor with cutter and two matchholders.

Sphinx cigar cutter. The body is cast iron and the cutter is brass. There is a Q on the cutter. 5" x 3".

This Bavarian architectural piece is wood with a beaded border around the base. It includes a humidor, cutter, and matchholder. The water pump is the cutter. 12" x 8".

Another desk piece in the Bavarian style, this has the cutter in the bird house. It is wood and brass with a beaded trim around the base. It includes a cigar cutter and rack, with a matchholder and striking surface. 9" x 11".

A beauty in rosewood and ivory, this desktop model has the cutter in the top of the tower. The fence around the back has holes for use as a cigar rack. A push of the ivory lever on top cuts the cigar. There is a striking surface framed in ivory at the front of the base, and two barrels for matches. 11" x 12".

Transportation & Nautical

This creative cutter takes the form of an early car. The steering wheel is pushed to cut the cigar. The headlights are amber glass. Marked "Germany" on the front bumper. 5" x 4.5".

This fanciful carriage is constructed of mother-of-pearl and metal. The ornate steering mechanism contains the cutter and around the back is a brass cigar rack. On top it is marked Muster Schultz. 9" x 4".

Baby buggy with cigar rest, and double cutter. Made of wicker, rubber, and brass.

An intricately designed die-cast cart on a wooden base. The cart is pulled forward to cut the tip. There is an attached metal striker. 5.5" x 6".

Bicycle shaped cutter with rubber tires and moving parts. The plunger cutter is located in the handlebar post. 8" x 6".

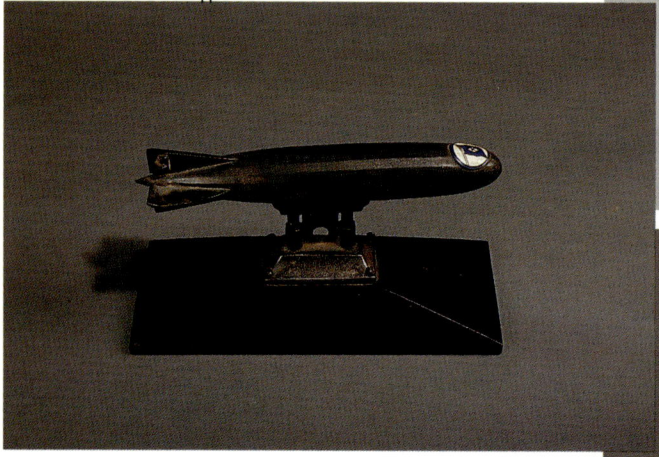

This blimp on a wooden base, with a blue flag bearing the letter "K" on top. The blimp is pushed down to cut the cigar. Metal, 7" x 4".

This tin airplane has a cutter behind the propeller operated by turning the prop. A matchbox is on top, cigarette holders in the wings, and a humidor in the fuselage. The propeller is marked D.R. G.M. Germany. 8" x 6" x 10".

"Odd or Even Cigar Cutter," cigar cutting made into a game. Turn the wheel to see which number will show up in the holes. Cast iron, 7.5" x 8".

Nautical cutters, ranging from 4.5" to 7.5" Second from left is marked "Compliments, Newfoundland, Canada Steamship Ltd., Halifax, Nova Scotia." In most, the cigar was placed in the top of post and the wheel turned to cut the cigar.

Cigar cutter and ashtray. Turn the nautical wheel, supported by two Oriental-style fish, to cut your cigar. 6" x 8".

A variety of ship wheel cutters. The third from the left is marked "Eingetr, Schultm...Elzit".

Ship wheel cutters mounted on ashtrays.

Six brass nautical cigar cutters in the form of ship's telegraphs. Lower level, center right: Ruckwarts, polished steel. Far right: Chas. Cory & Son, Inc. Patentees, New York. Top left: DRGM Arth. Lambrecht. Hamburg, top right: Lingern, Schultm...Elziz. All approx. 5" x 6".

Five souvenir ship wheel cutters. This were also bought as mementoes of a sea voyage. Left to right: S.S. Resolve, Made in Germany, Lingern, Schultm...Elzit; "Kronprinzossin Cecilie"; Milwaukee; Schultm...Elzit; D. "Hansa", Schultm...Elzit; D. "Columbus". All approx. 5" x 6".

This elaborate silver piano stool, includes not only a three-hole cutter, but a butler's bell, and snuff and matches sections in the seat. The cutter is in the post and is activated by turning. 9" x 8".

Below: Brass and other metals make up this unusual cutter, which is also a humidor. It is in the shape of a kitchen range and the top lever pulls up to reveal the humidor. The top left oven is the cutter, and underneath a drawer pulls out to empty the tips.

Right: Deeply embossed beer stein cigar cutter. The cigar goes in the top, which turns to cut. Brass plated, 1.5" x 3".

Above: Gun-shaped cutters. The center cutter is marked Muster Schutz.

Left: A delicately formed doll-sized chair. The top of the chair pulls up to reveal cutter blade. When not in use, there is a button on the side of the chair to lock the cutter into place. 1.5" x 4".

Handcrafted guillotine, brass and wood, 9" x 14".

A brass guillotine cigar cutter, with wooden base. 3.5" x 7.5".

Wood and metal guillotine cigar cutter, with a wicker basket behind to catch the tips, 3.75" x 10".

Handcrafted guillotine with fancy wire details. Brass and wood, 8" x 15".

Right: This cutter is in the form of either an insecticide sprayer or an old-fashioned, handheld fire extinguisher.

Top: This nicely formed brass cutter is a mouse-trap that closes down to act as a cutter. It is on a Bakelite base, on which also sits a brass potential prey. 2.75" x 2".

Above: Brass and wood water pump cutter. The cutter is on the top of the spout and is operated with the pump handle. The tip falls into the bucket which can be removed for emptying. Small hollow for ashtray.

A brass cigar cutter with a wooden base in the form of a hand pump. 6" x 9".

Padlock cutter.

Padlock cutter.

This silverplated post lamp is a combination cutter, ashtray, and kerosene lighter, with a glass lantern. Silverplate by Reed and Barton. 7" x 9".

In the center is a brass desk set consisting of a lady's shoe cutter on top of a humidor with a matchbox holder on the right and a cigar holder on the left. Two small metal shoe pushdown cutters of the same design are on either side. 10" x 4". The separate shoes are 4" x 3", with an engraved "Q" on top and "Regstr. 64" on side.

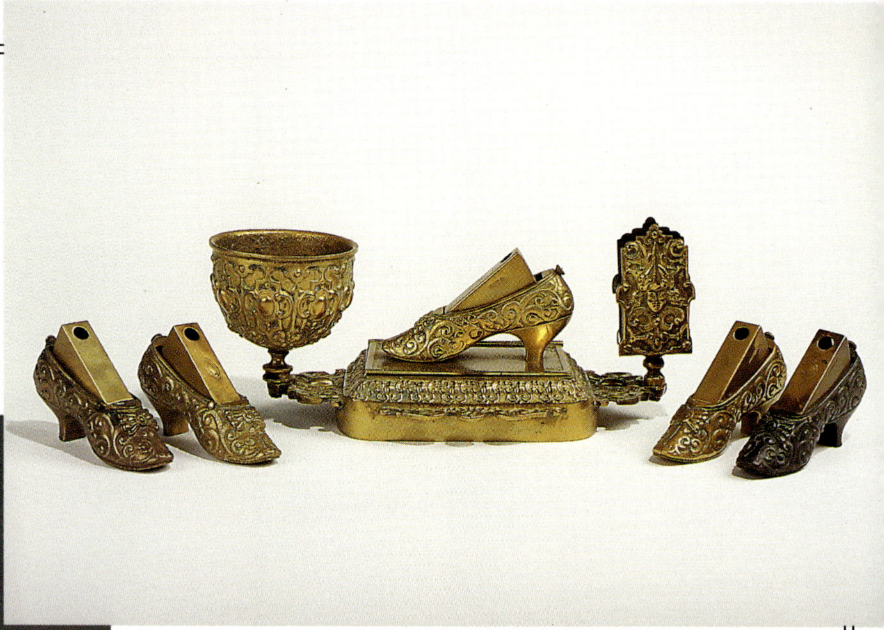

Cigar cutters in the form of woman's shoes. Left: 8.5" x 4"; middle: 4.5" x 2.5"; right: shoe with ashtray and matchbox holder, 8.25" x 4.25".

Wine bottle cutter.

Above Right: Four metal champagne bottle-shaped cigar cutters. Far left: brass, plunger mechanism, 3" x 7". Center left: cutter, striker, and matchsafe. Top opens up to reveal matchsafe. 3" x 9". Center right: cutter and matchsafe, 3" x 10.5". Far right: humidor, Woodland, Cook Co., quadruple plated. 3" x 9.5".

Right: The bottles disassembled.

Decorative Desk Cutters

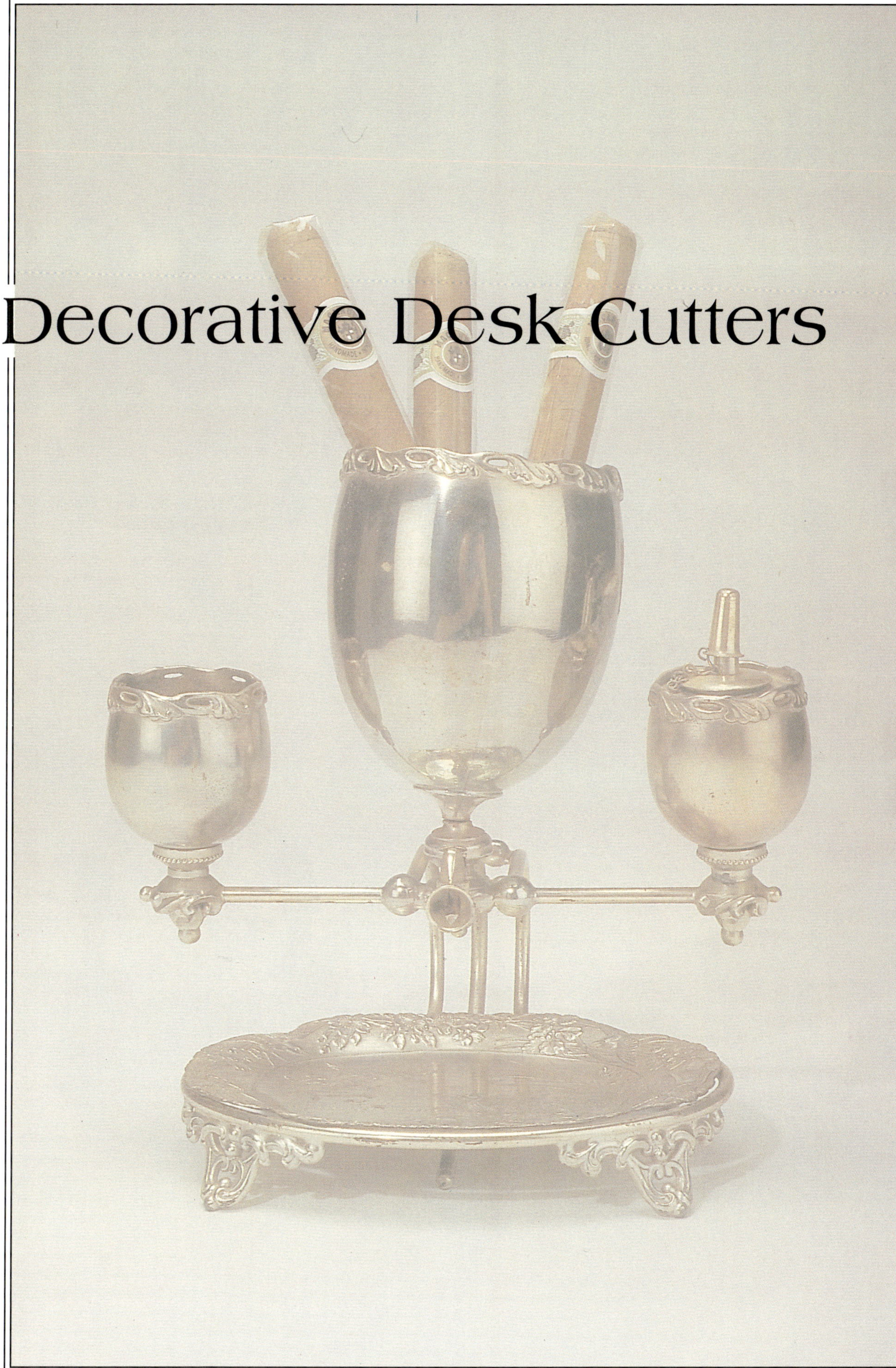

Right: Wood and brass cutter with matchholders and cigar rack. The scale on the pedestal may have been for a thermometer. 9" x 11".

Below Right: Although it has no cutter, this wooden cigar rack and matchholder with striker is quite attractive. 8" x 8".

Below Left: Brass cups and cutter sit atop a faux marble wooden base in this handsome desk set. 7.5" x 4.5".

Wooden desk set in the "tramp art" style. It contains a cigar rack, cutter, ashtrays, matchholder, and humidor. 11" x 8.5" x 11".

This wood and brass desk piece has a cutter, and cups for cigars and matches. 8" x 4".

German cast iron cutter, cigar holder, matchholder, 7" x 4". Marked "verleg bei E G Zimmerman in Hanay 12768."

Silverplated desk top cutter, kerosene lighter, ashtray, and cigar holder. No markings 7" x 8" x 6.

Three cutters in one cast iron Brunhoff base, patented Oct. 7, 1902, May 22 and Aug. 7, 1906. This may have been used in a cigar store or in a tavern or saloon. 13" x 5".

This desk piece is wood and copper. The cutter has three hole sizes, and there is a match cup and striking surface. 7" x 4".

A desktop set with matching candlestand and cutter/ashtray. Brass plated, 3" x 4" and 3" x 5".

A silverplated cigar cutter, matchbox holder, and ashtray sit atop a glass humidor. 6" x 9.5".

The mechanism for this cutter is in the hole in the candlestick pedestal. It is activated by pulling the top fin of the decorative fish handle forward. It has a matchholder with a striking surface, 5.5" x 3.5".

Iron and wood desk top electric lighter and cutter, with embossed cupid on the top, 7" x 5.5", Abbot Electric.

Iron cutter and matchbox holder, 2.5" x 4".

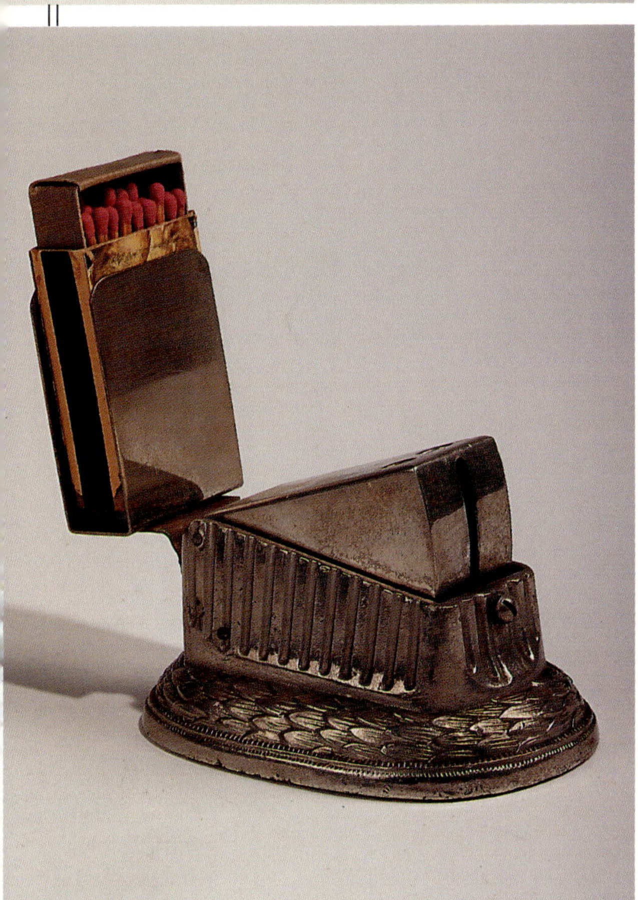

The Brunhoff label.

Pushdown cigar cutter with two holes, and matchbox holder. Paper label on bottom, Brunhoff Manufacturing Co., Useful Advertising Devices, 5" x 5".

Right: Cigar cutter and kerosene lighter. Brass and glass, 3.75" x 5".

Below: Brass cutter and kerosene lighter on a handpainted porcelain plate. The ball on top lifts to reveal the wick. 5" x 5".

This sterling silverpiece has a cutter in its handle and a kerosene lighter in the ball. The ball pivots as it is lifted to keep the flame upright. 4" x 2".

Plunger cutter with pushdown handle on a handpainted porcelain tray. There is a lion's head emblem on the top of the column. The plate is marked 6284 on bottom. 4.5" x 5.25".

Brass pushdown cutter and tray with two cigar rests. K & Co. on bottom. 5.5" x 2".

Cigar cutters with trays. Left: Sterling silver, one cigar rest, 4.5" x 3". Middle: Quadruple Flame, hard white metal, E.G. Webster & Son, 3.75" x 4". Right: Brass, slicing blade, three holes. 4" x 4".

Brass and wood ashtray with cutter, 5" x 2.75".

Desk top cutter and ashtray. 4" x 3.25", white metal marked "Quadruple Plate." E.G. Webster and Son, New York.

Brass cutter, ashtray, and matchbox holder, 7.5" x 6".

Copper ashtray and metal cylinder-shaped cutter. Round, 5" x 2".

Brass and hammered copper ashtray, cigar cutter, holder, and matchholder. The cutter is pleasingly shaped and cuts with a slicing motion.

Cobalt blue ashtray with silverplate fixtures and cigar cutter. A souvenir, it has a shield with the U.S. Congress building and the words "Capitol-Washington, D.C." 4" x 3".

Silverplate cutters. Right: Ashtray with cutter and kerosene lighter, H & H hallmark on bottom, 3" x 4.5.; Left: ashtray with matchholder and plunger cutter, 4" x 6".

The brass cutter and matchbox holder stand in the center of a glass ashtray. J.H. Astruck, New York, USA, Patented June 21st, 1910, June 3, 1913, etched into glass. 6" x 5".

Right: The brass cutter and a matchbox holder sit atop this glass pedestal. There are cigar rests on the brass rimmed glass ashtray at the base. The matchbox holder is embossed with two torches. 6.75" x 10".

A simple brass cutter and matchbox holder on a pedestal base. 3" x 4".

Tusk with nicely sculpted dog's head cutter with glass or gemstone eyes. It accommodates one size of cigar at the top of nose and one under it. The jaw pushes up to operate the cutter. 10" x 2".

Brass cigar cutter, with cigar rest, ashtray, and matchbook holder. 6" x 7".

A wonderfully crafted boar's head cutter on a boar's tusk. Elaborate metal trim runs to tip of tusk. 11" x 4".

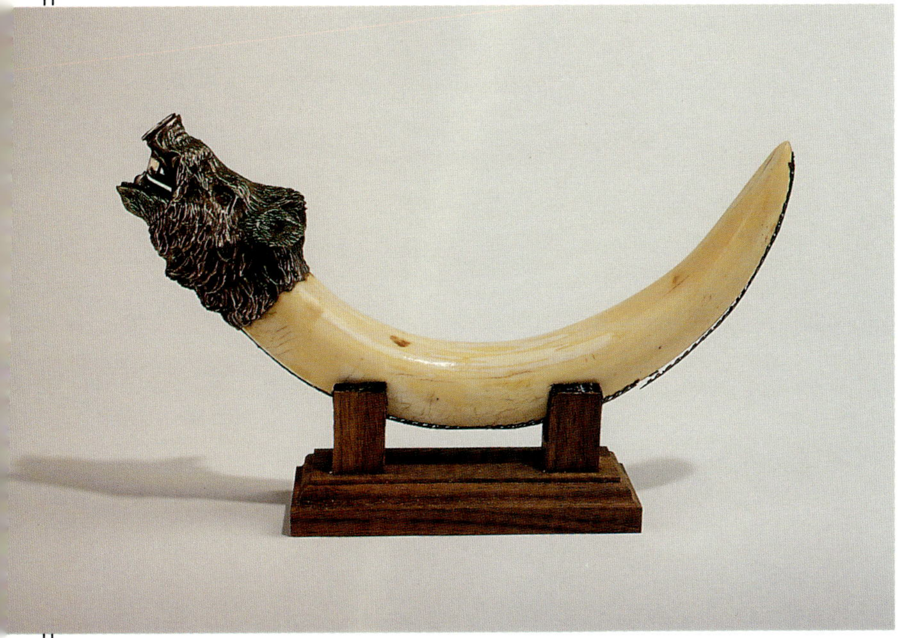

Three tusk cigar cutters, with metal cutters on one end. Front: two holes, and Sellenger, Germany hallmark on cutter, 6" x 2". Middle: three holes 8.25" x 3". Back: two holes, marked Germany, 925 on cutter, 2.5" x 10".

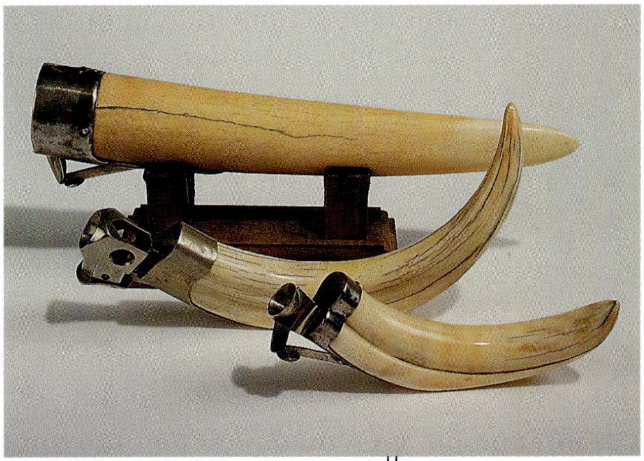

Beautifully rendered boar's tusk with boar's head cutter at the end. Similar to the dog cutter shown elsewhere, the eyes are glass or gemstone and it has two hole sizes for cigars.

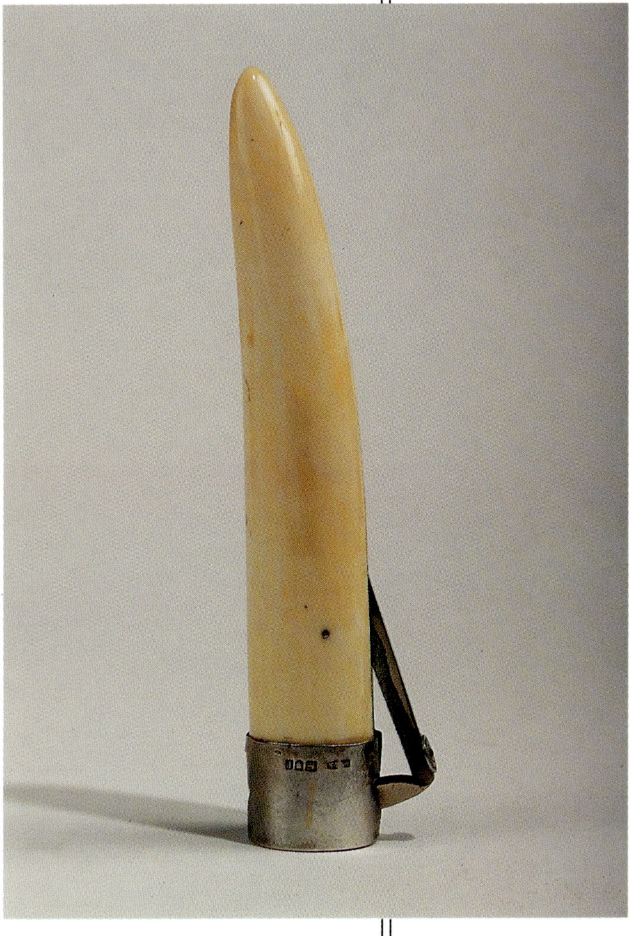

Tusk cigar cutter with two-hole mechanism inside the handle. A.S. hallmark. 7.5" x 1".

This pressed glass ashtray has a brass rim, candleholder and matchbox holder. An antler horn cigar cutter is attached across the rim. 11" x 11".

These deer antler pieces, a kerosene lighter and a cigar cutter, were produced after the 1920s. Left: 11.5" x 3"; right: 10" x 1.5".

Two horn-handled cutters, the metal cutters attached to their bases. Above is spirally textured antelope horn, 11.5" x 4", marked 5650-DBGM, Pfeilring /Solingen on cutter. Below: deer horn, 11" x 1.5".

Handcrafted cutter and kerosene lighter, with two small ashtrays. The body is a water buffalo horn and the metal work is silverplated brass. 14" x 11".

Antler horn cigar cutters. In most the metal cutter is attached to the base of the horn, but in the horn on the left, the cutter is contained inside and the cutting hole is in the end of the horn. Sizes range from 8" x 2" to 10.5" x 2".

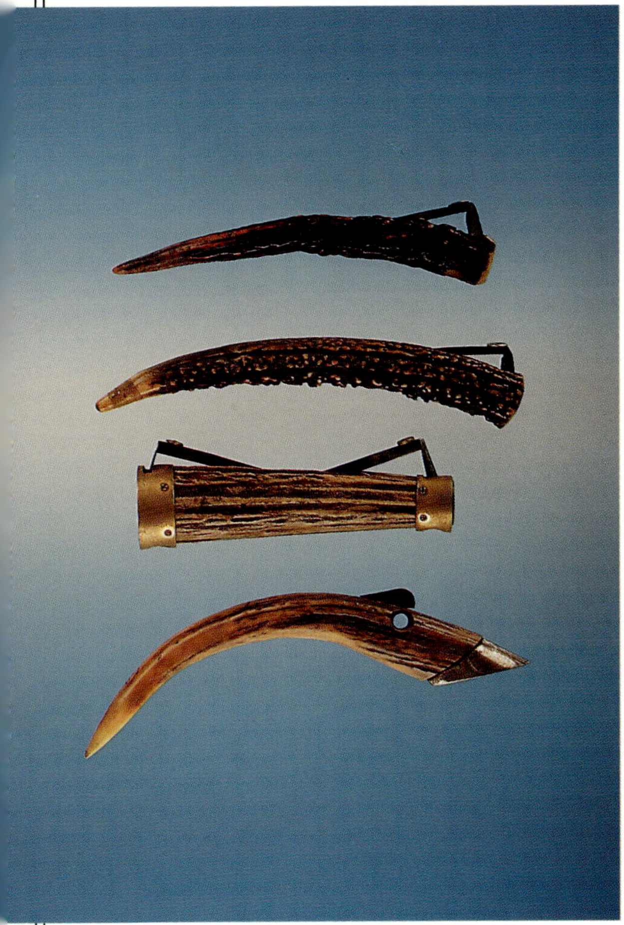

Antler cigar cutters. Notice the silver hoof on the end of the bottom cutter. 5.5" to 8".

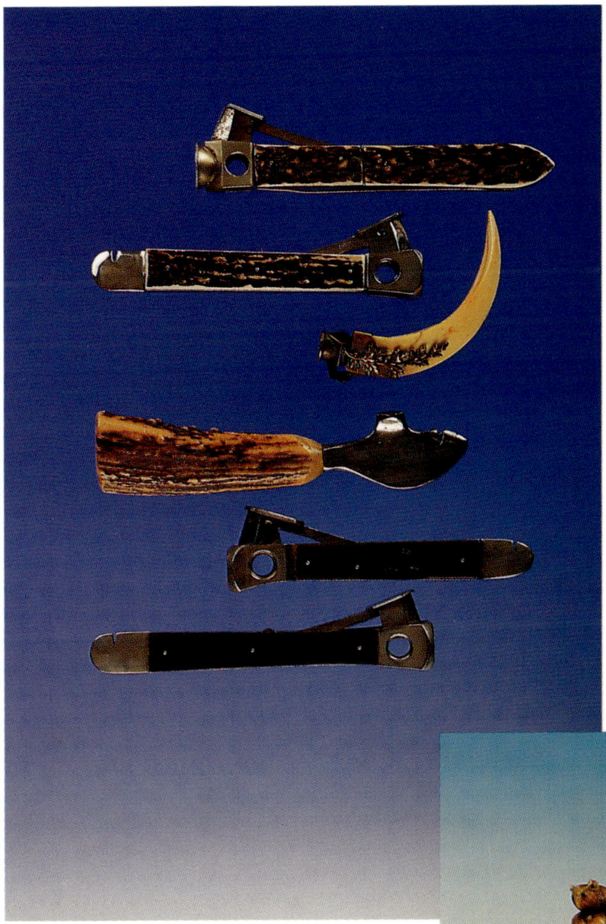

Cigar cutters and a cigar box opener, all with bone, tusk, or antler handles. 5" to 6".

Carved bone or ivory handles beautify these two desktop cigar cutters. The metal is sterling silver. 6.5" and 5.5".

The deeply relieved sculpting of metal cigar cutter is reflective of gothic revival architectural carving. It has holes of two sizes. 3" x 3.75".

The blade is in the body of this pump-like cutter. The handle activates it. Cast iron and brass. 5" x 4".

Desktop plunger cutter in cast iron.

Desktop cutters came in a variety of forms. Left: silverplate cutter and matchholder with ashtray, Derby Silver Birmingham, Conn., on bottom, 5" x 5". Middle: handled cutter attached to brass-rimmed glass tray, 5" x 3". Right: combination letter opener, knife, and cigar cutter, Magentic Cutlery Co., Phila., Pa, on base,, Vere Woodring & Co., Hazleton, Pa, D.R.G.M. on knife blade. 9" x 1".

Handcrafted cigar cutter using the range finder and stock of a real gun. The wood is marked 6811. 12" x 6".

Brass cigar cutter. Brunhoff Mfg. Co., base no. 18. 5.5" x 4.5".

An ornately sculpted brass cigar cutter with holes of three sizes. The bottom is marked W T & S. 4.5" x 4".

Below: Three pushdown cigar cutters. Left: brass, two holes. 2.5" x 3". Center: copper souvenir cutter for the Richest Hill in the World, Butte, Montana. 3" x 1.5". Right: K and Co. insignia on bottom, 3" x 1.5".

Above: Pushdown two-holed cigar cutters. Left: Q insignia, 3.25" x 3". Right: Made in London, 4" x 3.25".

Above Right: Art deco mask cutter in brass. This pushdown mechanism has a flat profile. 3" x 1.5".

Wood and cast iron cutter and matchholder, with three holes. 4.75" x 4". Pat'd July 18, 1887.

Bronze cigar cutter, footed. 7" x 4.5".

A nice brass and glass plunger type cutter. Push down top to cut the cigar. There are two hole sizes. 2" x 4".

Three brass plunger cutters with ashtrays. Left: 3" x 5". Middle: 5" x 7". Right: 3" x 3".

Art Deco styled plunger cutter with two hole sizes. 5.5" x 6".

Plunger brass cutter with holes for five cigar sizes. It is activated by pushing down the top. "Wm" mark on bottom. 5.5" x 9.5".

Fountain-shaped cutter, brass. 3.5" x 5".

Bakelite and iron cutter with plunger action, 2" x 5.75" x 4.5".

Rosewood and ivory cigar cutter, with plunger mechanism, shaped like town crier's bell. 2" x 4".

Metal cigar cutter, silvertoned, with two holes for cigars, push down the lever to cut. 4.25" x 7.25".

Brass cutters. Left: pedestal base, 4" x 3". Right: press-shaped cutter with two holes and a lift-out tray, 5" x 4.5".

Brass desktop cutters. Left to right: 2" x 5"; 3" x 4"; cutter on ashtray, 5.5" x 4"; large seashell ashtray and cutter, Muster Schultz on handle, 7" x 6".

Brass cutter, 3" x 6".

Metal urn-shaped cutter, with two holes. 4.5" x 4.25".

Three cutters. Left: pedestal ashtray with cutter two hole sizes. Brass, 3" x 4.5". Middle: Wooden base and barrels, a match-holder and humidor, with a cutter on top of the larger barrel in the shape of a man on a boat, two hole sizes. 7.5" x 7.5". Right: Cutter with a Bakelite handle and base. Ampere, Millivolt on bottom. 4.25" x 2.5".

Silver cutter by Kerr. The handle is a very ornate leaf pattern. A red seal for wax is at the opposite end of the cutter. Geschez. Geschütz. 1" x 3.5".

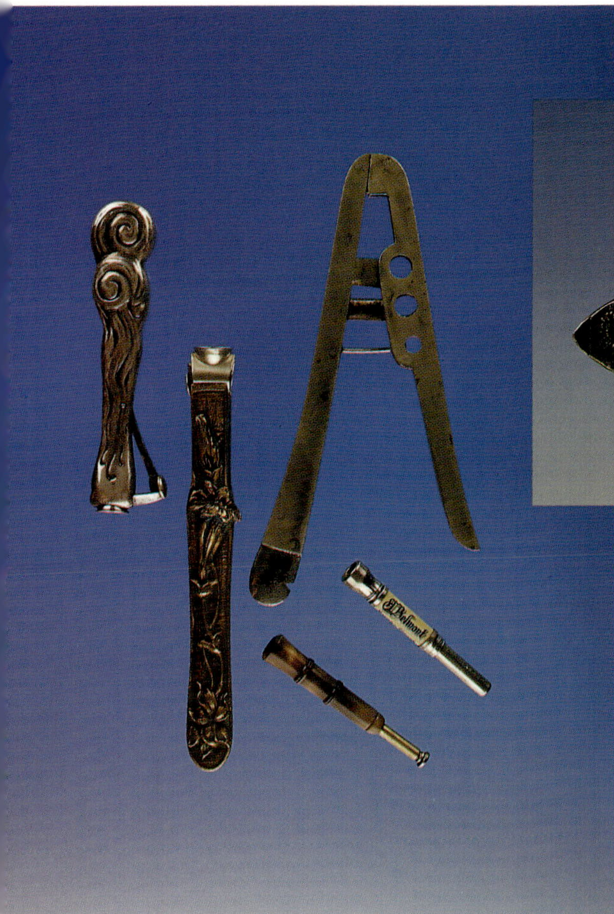

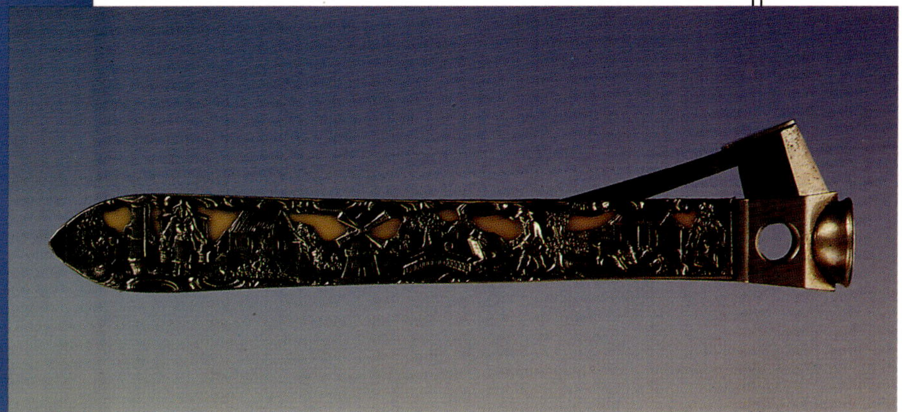

Close-up of one of the below cutters. Ivory or celluloid and engraved silver. Detailed Dutch scenes. 7" x .75".

Various desktop and vest pocket cigar cutters. One of the two telescope shaped pocket cigar punchers, bottom right, advertises St. Belmont Havana Cigars, "The New Kind", patented 1905, The Whitehead & Hoag Co., Newark, NJ, on celluloid. The other is made of Bakelite. The squeeze grip handled cutter at the top right has two holes and one puncher. The other two are Art Deco. 7.5" to 3".

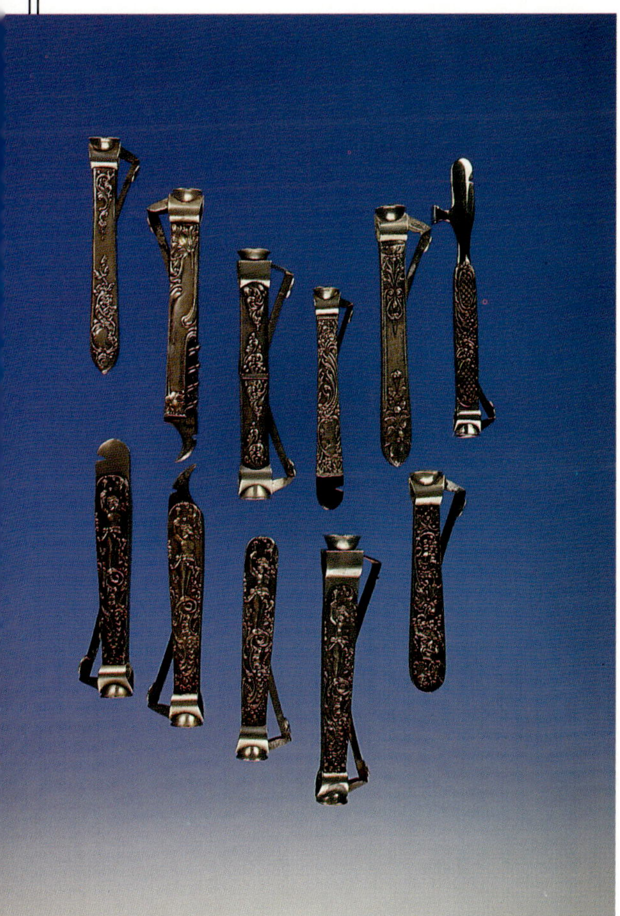

Embossed desktop cutters. All are about 5" long.

One embossed and four engraved cutters. All about 7".

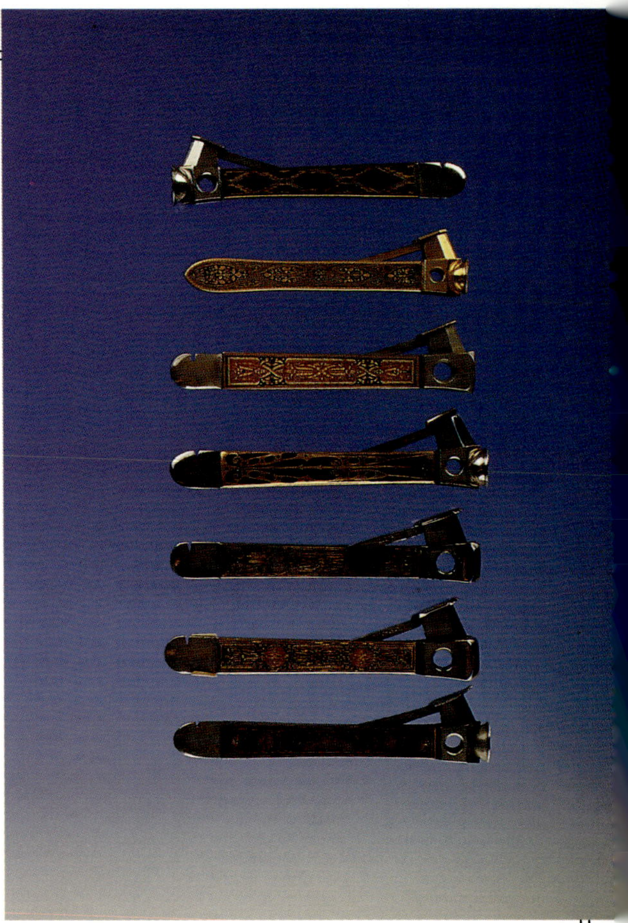

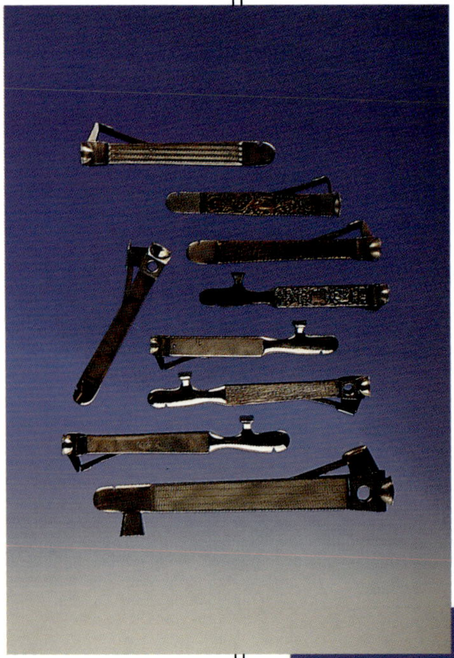

Right: German cloisonne cutters. All about 6".

Below Right: An assortment of hand held and vest pocket cutters. 1.5" to 5.5".

Left: Various engraved and embossed cigar box openers and cutters.

Below: Various desktop cutters and combinations of cutters and box openers. At the bottom are two silver and bone cutters. At the lower left is a small cutter, knife, and whistle, all attached by chains, which came in the red box above it inscribed Oscar Dahl, Kjöbenhavn. At the center right is a cutter that rests in a copper sheath. From 2" to 5.25".

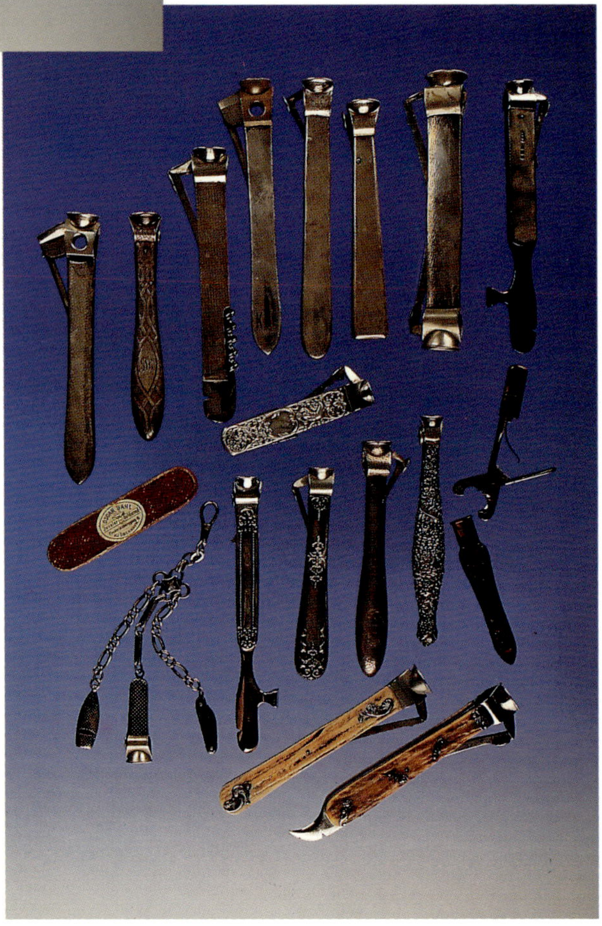

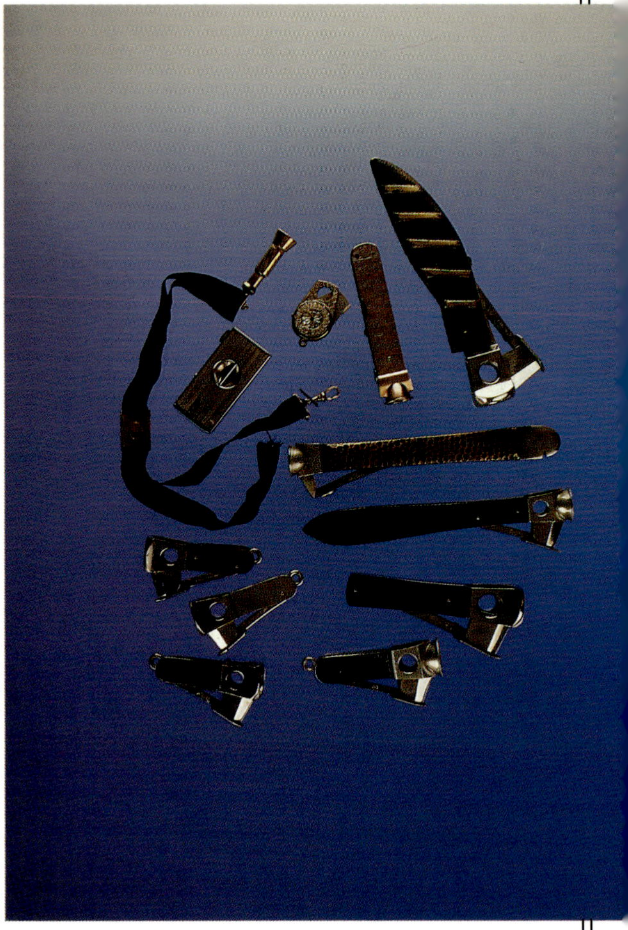

These three cigar cutters lead double lives. One is also a penknife, one also a broom, and one a box opener with a hand painted ivory handle. 8 to 3.5".

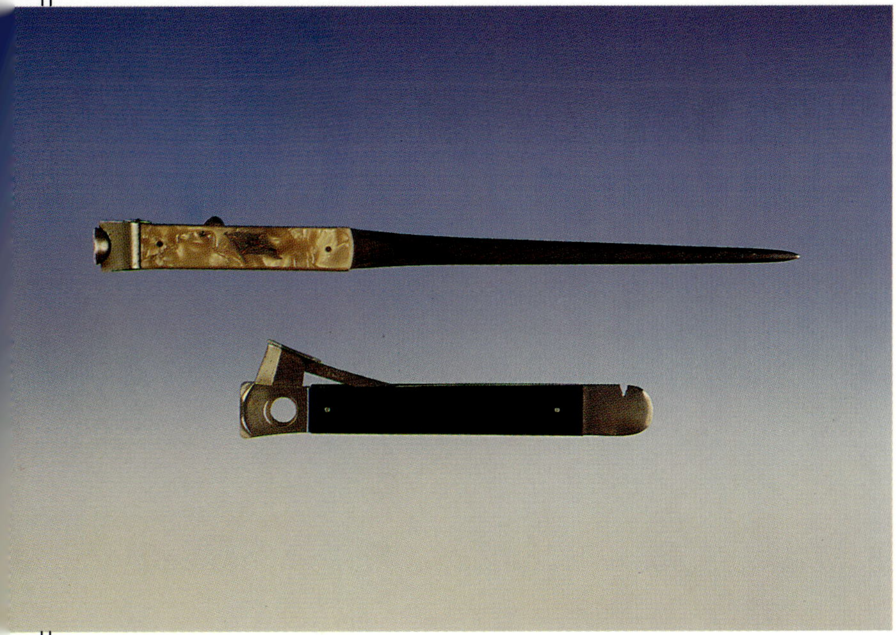

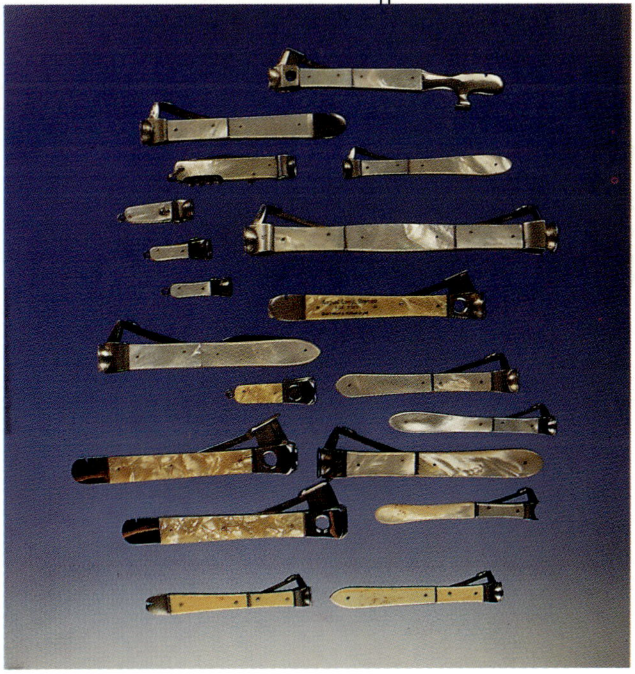

Above: Letter opener/cigar cutter with a silver flag bearing the letter N on it, 10" x 1". Bottom: Handheld cigar cutter and box opener. Solingen Donatus and Made in Western Germany on the cutter. 6" x 1".

Above Right: Handheld brass cigar cutter with two blades. The tooled panels have a turquoise stone and cover brass workings. Case marked Original Effwe Cellarius. 8" x 1".

Some of these desktop cigar cutters also have box openers. All have mother of pearl handles, except for the bottom two, which may be ivory. 8.5 to 4.5".

Right: Desktop cigar box openers; the notches are for pulling out the box nails and the hammer-heads to tap them back into place. Most are embossed silver or advertising pieces with celluloid handles. 4.75" to 6.5".

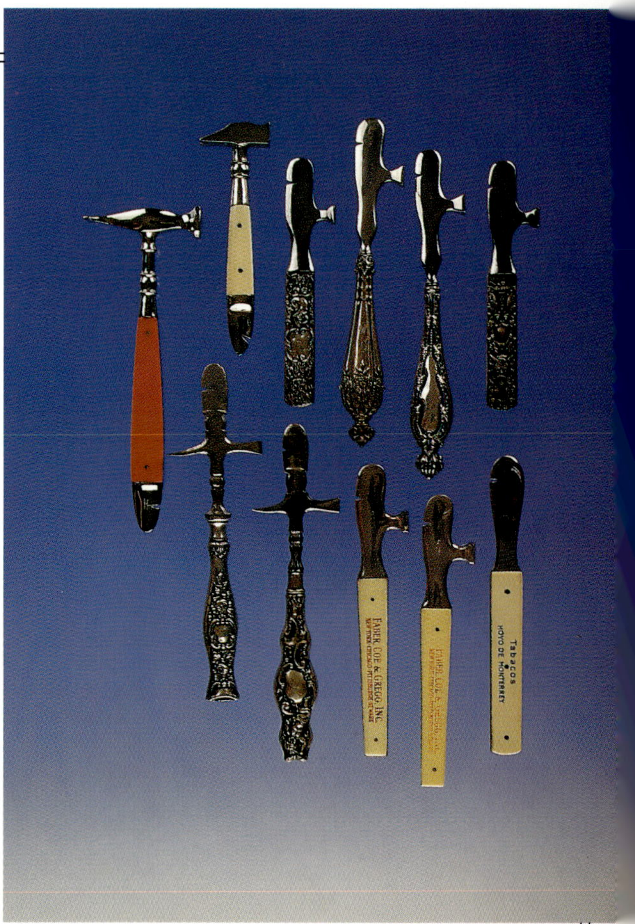

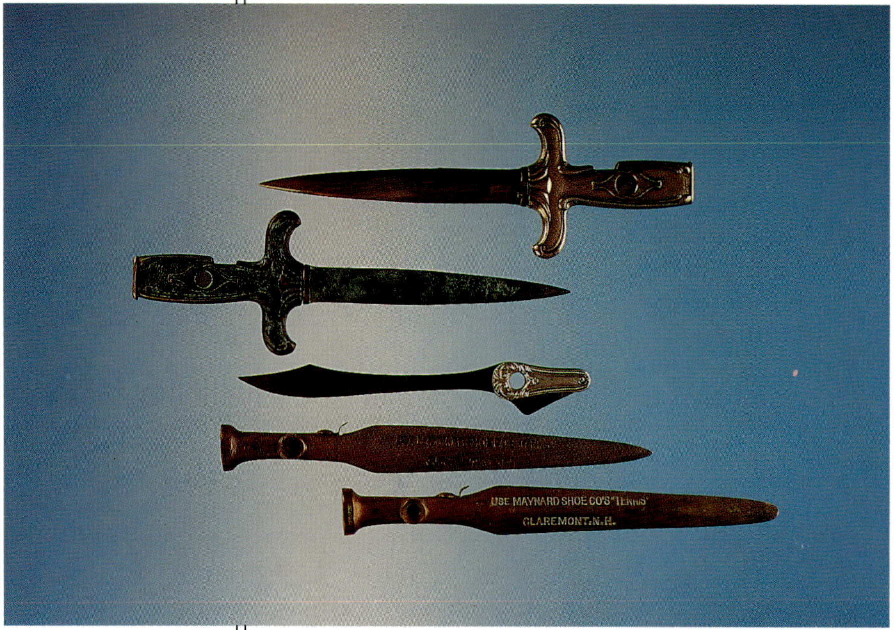

Letter opener cutters. The bottom two advertise "Use Maynard Shoe Co's 'Tennis', Claremont, N.H." The two dagger shaped cutters have blades that come off to reveal corkscrews. 8".

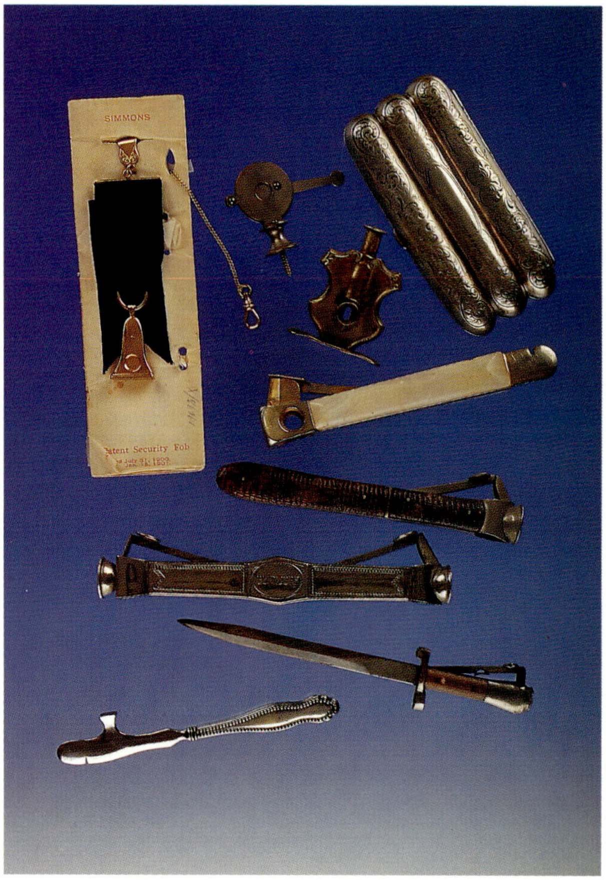

Desktop and vest pocket cigar cutters. At the top right is a pocket humidor, and at the top left is a watch fob cutter.

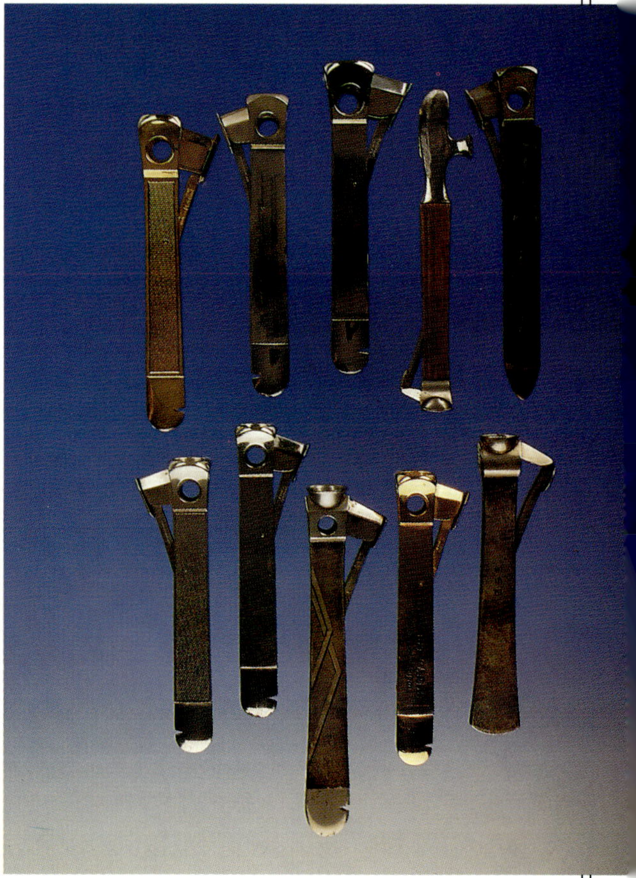

Engraved desktop cutters. All about 6".

Standing Cutters

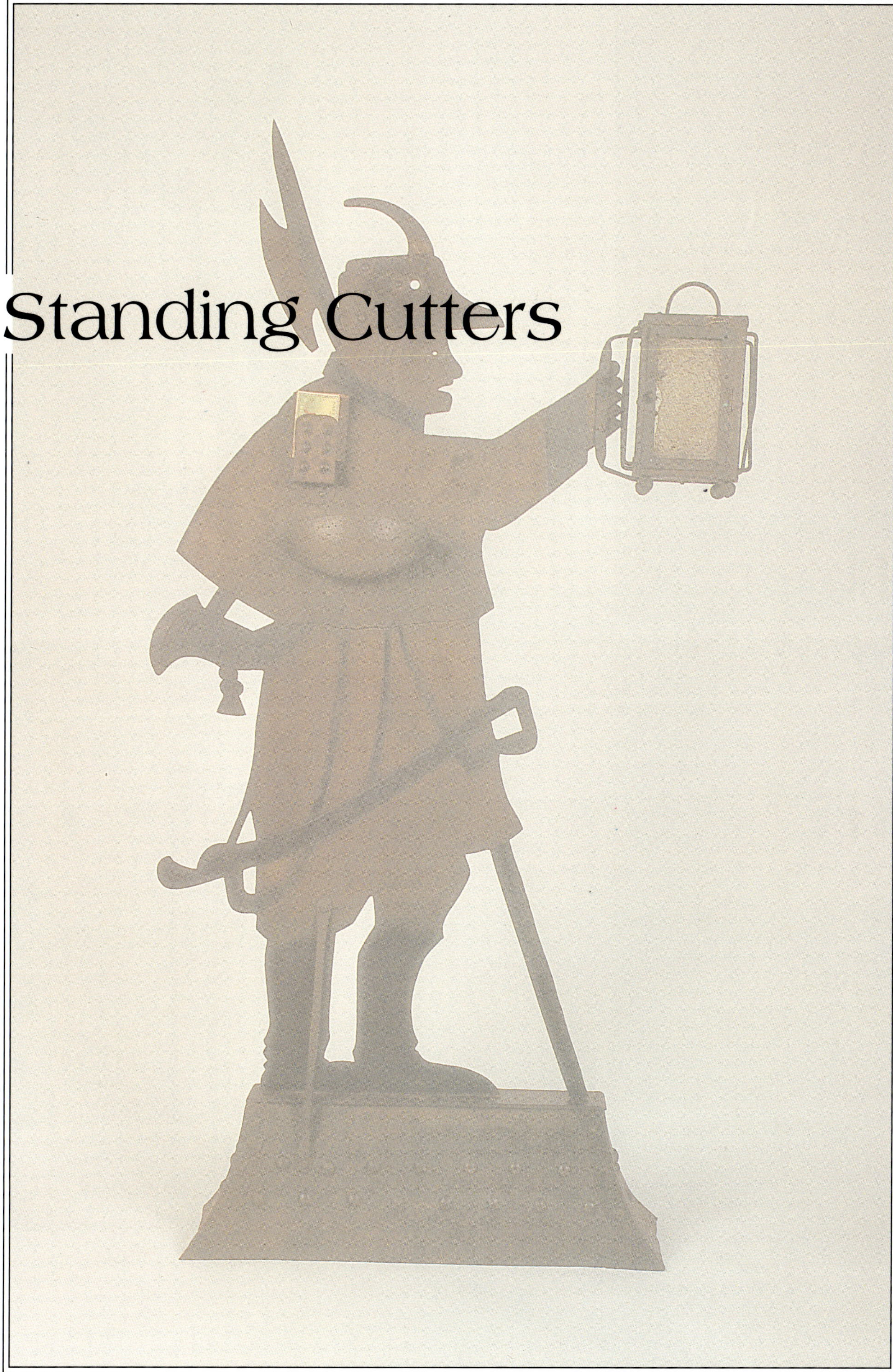

Left: Large metal bird with cast iron stand. The cutter is in the eye, and there is a candle that acts as a lighter, with a matchbox holder and an ashtray. 11" x 55.5".

Right: Sheet iron lantern, matchsafe, ashtray, and cutter. The cutter is under the plume of the hat. Made in England. 16" x 38.5".

Left: Similar to above; large cast iron bird which is a cutter, matchbox holder, candle lighter, and ashtray. 11" x 42.5".

Right: Sheet iron cutter, matchsafe, and ashtray. The cutter is in the mouth. When you pull the tail, the blade comes down, and the eyes "open." 7" x 41".

Vest Pocket Cutters

Left: Vest pocket combination cigar cutters and matchsafes. On most, the top has a lid which opens up to reveal a matchsafe, and the bottom is the cutter. At the bottom right is a cutter from 1876 World's Fair, Buffalo, New York, which is engraved on it.

Right: Vest Pocket cutters, mid to late 1800s.

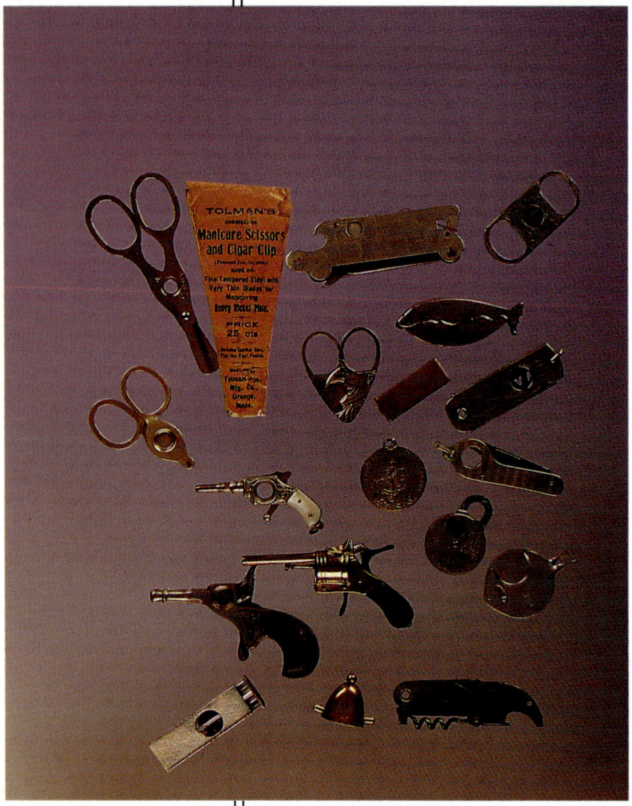

Left: Vest pocket cutters, mid to late 1800s.

Right: Vest Pocket cutters, mid to late 1800s.

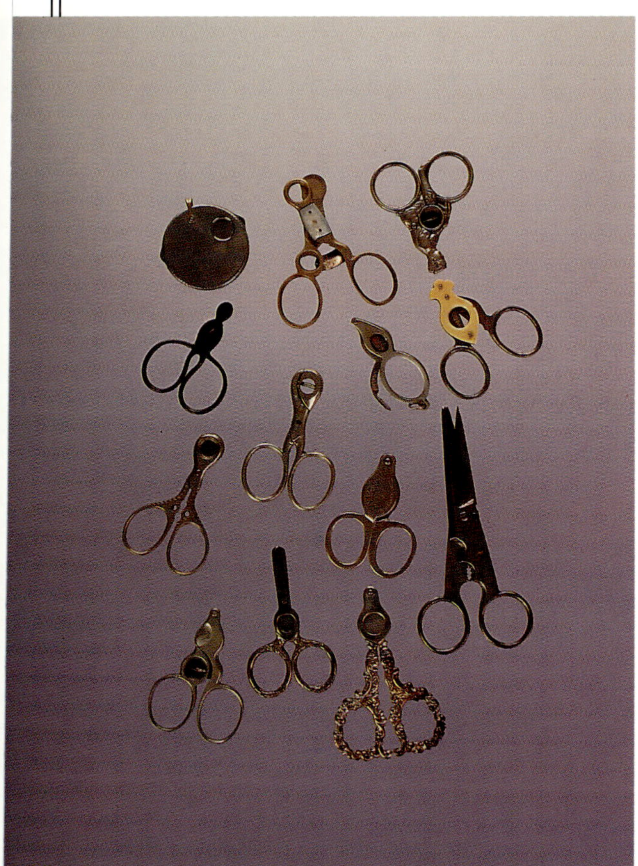

Vest Pocket cutters, mid to late 1800s.

People

Right: Metal kerosene or coal oil flint striker lighter. Nicely sculpted and marked Reynaldo on the pedestal. 7.5" tall.

For the huntsman there is this red-coated rider and his dog. Polychrome cast iron, the striker is in the tree and there is a striking surface on the wood base. Vistra, c. 1855. 7" x 4".

This kerosene lighter is in the form of a coppertoned bust with polished tooth necklace. The flame comes from the cigar. 4" x 7".

Bronze Indian striker lighter. Marked Austria. 6.75" x 7.5".

Right: Painted cast iron gas lighter featuring a woman figure playing croquet. 5" x 8.5".

This foppish fellow is a metal kerosene lighter. The flame comes from the cigar. 4.5" x 8".

Gargoyle coal oil lighter. The central plume of the head lifts to reveal a wick for the flame. The two side plumes are dips with small wicks for transferring the flame to the cigar. Bronze. 4" tall.

This bearded figure has a wick in his cigar, fed by a kerosene reservoir under the cap. 3" x 5".

Scotsman coal oil lighter. 2" x 4".

Devil's head striker lighter. The striking surface runs down the nose. Metal, 4" tall.

Right: Cast iron kerosene lighter. The base is a bird-like claw, with a devil's head top. The dip is a pitchfork between the horns, which is lighted at the wick on the end of the beard. 4" x 7.5".

Five "Hot Lips" lighters with an electrical device in the mouth to ignite cigars, 1920s. A switch on the bottom causes it to light when it is lifted, though the second Hot Lips from the left has the switch on the back. The third and fourth are marked "Pat. Applied For," and the fifth is marked "Hot Kiss" on the back

Electric lighter, sitting woman. The lighter heats when she is lifted. 3" x 6".

Electric lighter. White metal with bronze tone finish. 6.75" tall.

Right: Brass Punch gas lighter and matchsafe.

Coppertone "Hot Lips" electric cigar lighter. Automatic switch on bottom so it turns on when picked up. 6" x 8.5"

Coppertone cast iron "Hot Lips", Pat. Apr., 6" x 8.5".

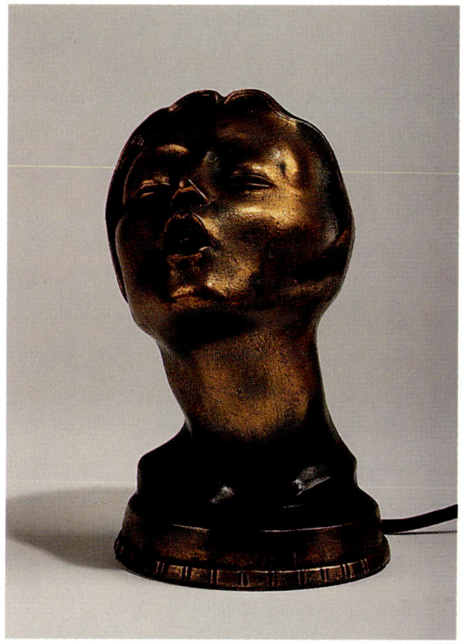

W.C. Fields electric lighter with red nose switch which is pushed to activate the lighter on the top of the hat. Patented Oct. 6, 1906, "Cabby Jed," Tramp Art. Copyrighted by Frankart, Inc. 4" x 5".

Coppertone "Hot Lips," 6" x 8.5". Automatic switch.

Iron "Hot Lips" with painted red tongue, switch on neck, signed Arturaferri. 6" x 8".

This electric lighter should hang on the wall. The lighter is in the pipe, but there is also a bulb behind the face which lights the eyes. Brass and wood. 9" x 9".

Animals & Birds

Brass full figural bear with matchholder and ashtray.

Above: Elephant striker lighters. The coppertone elephant is 2.75" tall; the silvertoned one is 5.5" tall with black Bakelite base and ivory Bakelite tusks.

Left: Ronson ape lighter/ashtrays. Marked 8864. 4" tall.

Below: A switch on the bottom activates this electric lighter when it is lifted. The lighter is in the middle of the monkey's banjo, which reads Auag 200/240 V. 2.5" x 6".

Elephant head lamp coal oil lighter. The wick in the trunk is lighted and a dip beneath the hat transfers the flame. 3" tall.

Bronze gas lighter with wooden base, in the shape of a lion fighting a serpent, whose tongue acts as the flame, 11" x 9".

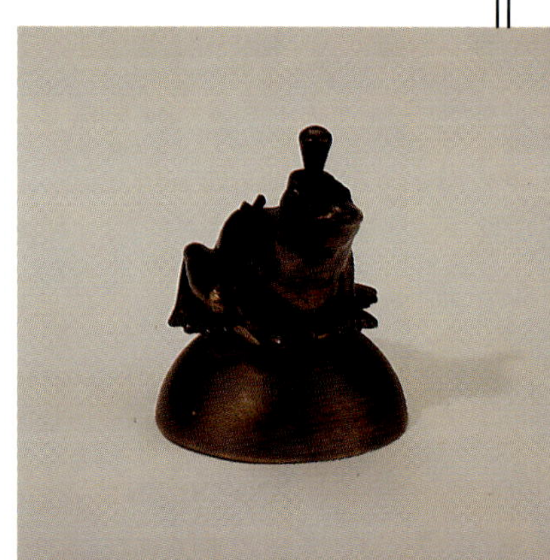

Frog on half sphere striker lighter. 3.5" tall.

Left: Handcrafted kerosene lighter, brass with a water buffalo horn. 11" x 4".

Right: Comic horse lighter with electric filament in the base. It has a built-in switch that engages when the animal is turned up for lighting. 5" tall.

Copperplated quail kerosene lighter. 3.5" x 6".

Above: Art deco horse head striker lighter. 4.5" tall.

Above Right: Copperplated horse head lighter. The eyes are colored glass. 4.75" x 7".

Right: Crow-shaped striker lighter. Japanned. 5.25".

Crow-like striker lighter. Art Metal Works, Newark, New Jersey, 5.25".

Other Objects

Right: Handgun-shaped lighter, marked "Modern Angel Mascot," Japan. 4" x 3".

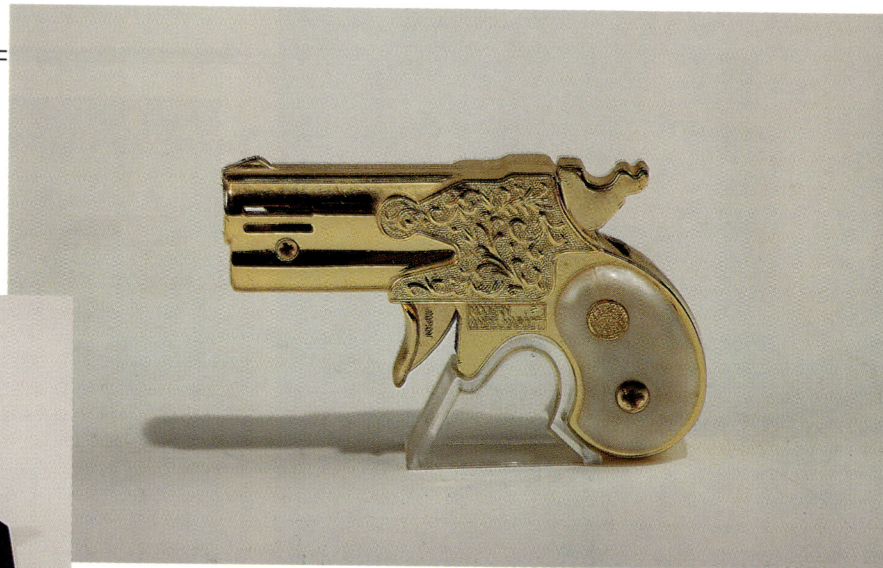

Top: The Spirit of St. Louis lighter by Swank. Made in Japan. Brass sitting on a wooden base. The lighter is activated by spinning the propeller. Total height 2.5", width 6.5".

Middle: These microphone electric lighters are reminiscent of the golden days of radio, circa 1920s. Left: 9" tall, right 5.5" tall.

Above: Three lamppost alcohol lighters. Left: chromeplated, glass lantern, 3" x 9". Middle: Brass, "Mr" on bottom, 3" x 10". Right: Brass, top pulls out with pull chain to light. 3" x 10".

Middle: Brass and wood gun-shaped lighter on a wooden base. K and Japan on trigger. 5.5" x 3".

Above: Hand grenade lighter lights by pulling the pin. Circa 1940s. 4.5" tall. Marked "Combat / P.G.L. / D. Pat. 14210."

Right and Below Right: Aladdin's lamp kerosene lighter. The flame in the spout stayed lighted while the three dips at the center could be used to transfer the flame. 5" tall by 6" wide.

Below: Glass kerosene wallhanging lighter with colored glass globe. The brass band around the reservoir is pierced.

Two brass kerosene lighters with glass globes. Stillman Safety Pat. Aug. 19-02 on handle. 8" x 6".

Ronson table top cigarette case and lighter, wood and brass. Tambour top. The coal oil dip on the right is used to depress the center button, generating a spark, which ignites it. 3" x 5.25" x 6".

Brass and copper kerosene desk lighter. The flame remains lighted. 6" x 2".

Below Right: Casco Electric Cigar Lighter, Bakelite and chrome. Connecticut Automotive Specialties Co., Bridgeport, Connecticut. 4" tall.

Below: Cigarette case and electric lighter. The Bakelite base has a lighter unit in the center surrounded by holes to hold cigarettes. The chrome dome has a Bakelite handle. 4.5" tall, 3" diameter. Circa 1920s.

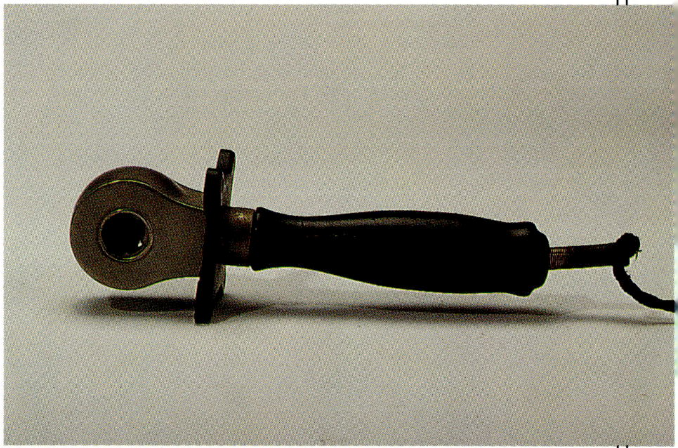

Handheld electric lighter with wood handle. Manning-Bowman & Co., Meriden, Connecticut.

Pair of green glass electric lighters, circa 1930. 3" tall.

Swirl glass globe electric lighter, circa 1930. 3.25" tall.

A patriotic matchsafe with two American flags, American eagle, and profile of Teddy Roosevelt in center. Cast iron, 6" x 11".

Pair of French matchbox holders with striking surface on cast iron base, Depose. Gambling pieces, 6" x 13".

Manning-Bowman table lighter, electric, 6.75".

AT THE STORE

This terra cotta dog with hat is smoking a cigar which is the gas lighter. 7" x 18".

II

Keywound Advertising Cutters

Equity Cigars, "Justice to All," A.S. Goodrich and Co., Milwaukee, Wis. Cast iron with 77 incised on bottom, 6.5" x 3.75".

Flying Dude, Boston Cigar and Tobacco Co. Cast iron mechanical cutter with revolving advertisement, 7.5" x 4". When you press the lever, a different logo appears in the window.

Reid & Co's Success mechanical cutter with key. Reid Tobacco, Milton, Pennsylvania. Cast iron, Brunhoff MFG. Co., Pat. March 5, 1901. 5.5" x 4.5".

Cutter for Barrymore Cigars, F.P. Norton & Co., Factory, Boston. Erie Specialty, Feb. 19, 1889. 4" x 5".

Gen. Sullivan Cigars, "Rich Good Fragrant", Jones Bros. Elec. Co., Cinn., Ohio 3.5" x 4.5". 94 incised on bottom.

Right: King Parrot Cigars, Morrisson Plummer and Co., Chicago, Cast iron, 5.5" x 3".

Below: Keywound mechanical cutters, 5" x 4". Left: Austin Nichols & Co.'s Improved Whip Handle. Right: Goldey Cigar, Goldsmith Silver & Co., Boston, Mass.

Straiton and Storms, Robert Burns Cigars, 3.4" x 4.5".

Embossed cast iron cutter for Loreto. 94 marked on bottom. 4" x 4".

Sprague, Warner and Co. Londres Cigars, 4" x 3.5".

Left: Barnett's Perfection, M.H. Barnett Maker, Springfield, Mass. 5.5" x 3.25", Erie Specialty Co.

Below: Three cast iron cigar cutters, all 5" x 4". Left: General Mansfield; middle: Chancellor Cigars, Wm. A. Stickney Cigar Co., St. Louis; right: Robert Bruce Cigars, J.H. Newins & Son, Riverhead, N.Y.

Three mechanical cutters with keys. Left to right: Estabrook and Eaton, Boston. 5" x 4"; Prize Winners and Union Blend Cigars, Geo. S. DeForest & Sons, St. John, N.B. 5" x 4"; Acker, Merrall & Condit Co. Brunhoff, 5" x 4".

Fidler's El Rocco Cigars, H.F. Fidler & Co Makers. 5" x 3.25", Brunhoff.

Round Top Cigars, Dearstyne Bros., Albany New York. 5.5" x 3.5", Erie Specialty.

Right: C.A. & S., Union Made, 5" x 3", Erie Specialties.

Below Right: Michael Katz spring driven cutter. Cast iron, Brunhoff Mfg. Co., 6" x 4".

Below Right Bottom: Cigar cutter with advertisement for Briar Pipes. 6" x 3.25", Erie Specialty, Pat. Feb 19, 1889.

Three Eisenlohr's Cinco Cigars cutters, Philadelphia. Cast Iron, Brunhoff Mfg. Co., 4" x 5".

Cast iron mechanical cutters. Left: Goldsmith Silver & Co., M.C.A., Boston. 5" x 4". Right: Lipschutz's 44. Marked 122 on bottom, 7" x 4".

Mechanical, keywound cutters. Left: Barry Lyndon Cigars, "Sweet Fame is Mine." 7" x 5", cast iron with 156 incised on bottom. Brunhoff. Right: Robert Burns Cigars, Geo. L. Storm & Co., New York. 6" x 5". Erie Specialty, Feb. 19, 1889.

Pierce's Nine Cigars. Erie Specialty, Pat. Feb 19, 1889, model 89, 6" x 3.25".

Below: Elindio Cigars, C & H Co. Brunhoff, 7" x 3". No. 129.

Below Left: Cutter advertising the Star Electric Co., Waterloo, Ind. 7" x 3". Given out as gratuity.

Bottom Left: Cast iron mechanical cutters. Left: "Golden Wedding." Right: Optimates Justin Seubert, Syracuse, N.Y. Both 6" x 4". Erie Specialty, Feb. 19, 1889.

A three dimensional cast figure of a coachman graces this hand painted cast iron cutter with mechanical key. The script advertises Touchlight Cigars, Mellow 5 Cents. 7" x 8".

Spring-driven keywound cutter for Red Hill Cigars. Cast iron.

La Sinceridad cigar cutter. The picture frame like stand has a marquee for advertising and a cutter in the top. Brunhoff, 9" x 6".

Cast iron cutter advertising Omar cigars, Barnes, Smith and Co. 5" x 4.25".

Below: Cast iron cutter with painted base, 4" x 5".

Above: Two cast iron Counsellor cigar cutters. Philadelphia. Allen R. Cressman's Sons, Brunhoff Mfg. Co., 6" x 4".

Above Right: Two cast iron cutters with mechanical keys. Left: Waitt & Bond Blackstone. Right: copperplated, P & M cigars, Brunhoff, 7" x 5".

Right: Left: Cast iron cutter for Robert Burns cigars, "Try One." Geo. L. Storm & Co., New York. 5" x 4.25". Right: Cast iron cutter, The Bachelor, 5" x 4.25".

Wood and brass barrel-shaped two hole cigar cutter with striking surface. It advertises Abercrombie & Co., Boston, Metropole, pat. Mar. 10, 91.

Below: Wood and metal treasure chest shaped cigar cutter. On top it reads "'Old Chest,' A Treasure of a Smoke." 6.75" x 4.75".

Below: Cast iron clock and cutter for Three Brothers Cigars, Frings Cigars. 8" x 12.5" x 6", Brunhoff.

Cast iron cutter featuring George Washington for Continental Cigars. 8.5" x 15.5", Brunhoff Mfg. Co., Cincinnati, Ohio.

Above Left and Left: Cast iron cigar cutter, Artie Boy. There is a wind-up lever on the side to power the cutter. When you pull down the man's arm, his tongue comes out to spit out the tip. Erie Specialty, pat. Feb. 19, 1889.

Right: "Muriel" cutter, 5.2" x 8.5", The Brunhoff Mfg. Co., circa 1920s.

Below Right: Left: Traiser's Harvard cutter, 4.5" x 8.5", Brunhoff Mfg. Co., circa 1900s-1930s; right: humidor of same brand 7.5" x 8.5" x 11". A bell rings when the box is opened, c. 1900s-1930s.

Top: Rocky Ford cutter, 8.5" x 4.5", Brunhoff, c. 1900s-1930s.

Middle: Judge Fair cutter, 8" x 4.5", round base, Brunhoff, c. 1900-1930s.

Above: BCA Keystone cutter, 8" x 4.5", Brunhoff.

Captain Alvarez cutter, 4.5" x 8.5", c. 1900s-1930s.

John Hay cutter, 8" x 4.5, Brunhoff.

Q & Q Perfecto cutter, Quinn Bros. Manufacturers. Brunhoff.

Las Amantes, 8 X 4.5", Havana Cigars, D.S. Erb and Co., Brunhoff.

Peter Schuyler cutters with three different logos, each 8" x 4.5". G.W. Van Slyke and Horton Cigar Manufacturers. Cutter by Brunhoff.

This mechanical cutter has a wind-up drive. It is tin and wood with reverse painting on glass advertising Muriel Cigar, Costello Bros, Inc. Distrs., Pawtucket, Rhode Island. 11.5" x 5".

Above: Tin cutter with wooden base, wind-up mechanism. The reverse painted glass marquee advertises reads Mozart Cigars. 11.5" x 5".

Above Left and Left: Inner workings of standard mechanical cigar cutters, front and back. The shell is normally reverse painted on glass or applied decal on glass.

Pushbar Advertising Cutters

Right: Flor de Manuel Cigars. Glass and iron cutter with pushbar, 6" x 3".

Below Right: Wood and brass cutter, with pushbar and three holes of varying sizes. It advertises Iraba cigars, by A. Fader and Son, Baltimore, 8" x 4.5".

Top: Pair of cast iron cigar cutters with pushbar in front and three sizes of cigar holes, both 3.25" x 3.25". Left: Smokettes, Always the Best, the Leland & Smith Co. Sole Accents, Toledo, Ohio. Right: Gold Medal Cigars the J.C. Orrick & Son Co., Cumberland.

Above: Two tin and wood with pushbar cutter. The marquees are paper under glass and advertise Rigby's Argo Club and Marie Antoinette. 8" x 4.75".

Y-B cutter with clever "B-Ys and Buy Y-Bs" slogan on glass. 8" x 4.5", brass with lever pull on front to operate cutter, Brunhoff, Cinn., Ohio.

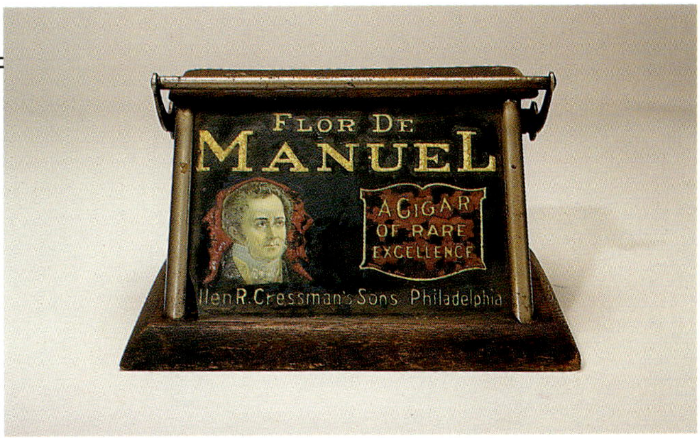

Above: Tin and wood cutter with pushbar for Flor de Manuel, Allen R. Cressman Sons, Philadelphia. 8.5" x 5.5".

Left: Wood and brass cutter, with pushbar lever, advertising Rose-O-Cuba Cigars, John K. Thomas & Co. 8" x 4.5"

Left: Four cast iron cutters with glass marquee and pushbar. Left to right: Flor de Melba, Fring 3 Bros Cigars, Charles Denby Cigars, Flor de Manuela, 6" x 3".

Bottom Left: Lever driven cast iron cutter for Neudecker's Own. Wooden base. 3" x 4".

Below Left: Three tin and wood cutters with side levers. Left to right: Victory, W.C. Fruitiger & Co; The New Currency, P. Lorrilard Co., Donovan & Bressler; Texas, Marque Deposse F.L. The Victory and New Currency cutters have reverse painted marquees, while the Texas marquee is paper under glass. 8" x 4.75".

Tin and wood cutters with pushbars. Top: Fleur de Manuel , Allen R. Cressman's Sons, Makers, Philadelphia, (reverse on glass); left: Topic, Stein Bros., Milwaukee, Wisconsin (paper label); Strongheart (paper label). All are 8" x 4.75".

Paper under glass marquees advertise Javotte Havana Cigars and Boston Trade, Chas. Odence, in these tin and wood cutters with side levers. 8" x 4.75".

Pushdown Advertising Cutters

Left: This figural piece features a three-dimensional sculpted prince or page and advertises Coronet Cigars. Metal, Brunhoff Manufacturing Company, Advertising Specialties, no. 850B on bottom. 5.5" x 6.5".

Left: Rocky Ford Cigar, cutter and match dispenser with striker on front. Cast iron, 6" x 7", marked 177b, Brunhoff.

Below: Punch's mouth is the cutter on this deeply sculpted piece. It advertises Tansill's Punch. Cast iron, marked No. 78 on bottom. 5.5" x 3.5".

Pastora Cigar cutter and match dispenser, San Telmo Cigar Mfg. Co., Detroit, Michigan. Brunhoff, model 177B, marked on bottom, 5" x 9".

This Red Lion cutter is nicely cast in iron. Above the lion's head it reads "I am the King." Red Lion, Heyman Bros & Lowenstein Makers N.Y.. The base is marked No. 78 on bottom. 5.5" x 3.5".

Right: Snowbird Cigar cutter and match dispenser. Allen and Dunning Co., Paterson, New Jersey. 5" x 9", Brunhoff Advertising Specialties, cast iron.

Right: Cremo Cigar cutter and match dispenser with advertising marquee. 5" x 9", Brunhoff.

Below: Poet Cigar cutter with two holes. Brunhoff, Model No. 18, 5.5" x 3.5".

Above Left: Cast iron cutter and match dispenser for White Knight. Brunhoff Mfg. Co., 6" x 8.5".

McCahan's Cigars, Troy, New York. Iron with wood base, 3" x 3.25".

Pushdown cigar cutter for Geo. Bassett, 127 State St. Boston, Wholesale Cigars & Tobacco. 3" x 4".

Steel pushdown cigar cutter, with three holes. "Compliments of Morey & Meyers Cigar Co." on top. 4" x 4".

Left: The cast marquee is for M.C.A. Cigars. Cast iron cutter, Brunhoff Mfg., patent August 7, 1906, 4" x 7.5".

Below; Teeter-totter metal cutter, S.D. Ache & Co., Dealers in Fine Cigars, Pittsburgh, Pennsylvania. 8.25" x 3".

Davenport Cigars, Harkert Cigar Co. This has a rotating logo which turns when the cutter is engaged to reveal a second advertising marquee. Model No. 262, 5" x 7.5", Brunhoff.

The beautiful polychrome marquee of this cutter is for John C. Herman & Co.'s King Oscar Cigars. Brunhoff Mfg., patent August 7, 1906, 4" x 7.5".

Right: Estabrook & Eaton Fine Cigars, Boston, Cast iron cutter operated by pushing down surface. 4.75" x 7".

Below: Two views of a brass pushdown advertising cigar cutter. On the top is an engraving of a baby with the phrase "One consolation, your business." "Grammes" on cutter. Bottom: Made by L.F. Grammes & Sons, Allentown, PA, USA, 3" x 1.5".

Pushdown cutter advertising Acme. Erie Specialty. 3" x 4".

Cutter advertising Tadema Cigars, I. Samelson & Co. Distributors. Brunhoff Mfg. Co., August 7, 1898. 4" x 8".

The framed marquee of this cutter advertises Peter Schuyler Cigars. Cast iron, Brunhoff Mfg., patent August 7, 1906. 4" x 7.5".

Automatic Advertising Cutters

Free Lance cigars, Nicholas Kuhnen Cigar Co., Davenport, Iowa. Patented Oct. 7, 1902, 6" x 8", Brunhoff.

The working part of Brunhoff's cast iron model 216. With a marquee added this base is used in many of the automatic advertising cutters Brunhoff produced. 4.5" x 4.5".

Cast iron cutter for CTA Stubs cigars, Little & Hulett. Brunhoff base 216, 6.5" x 9".

Lawrence Barrett Havana Cigars, T. Rosenbaum & Co., Boston. 6.5" x 8", Brunhoff. 216 base.

Brown Beauties, P.N. Jacobsen, Jr. Maker. This is the Brunhoff model 216 with the marquee, patented Oct, 7, 1902. 6.5" x 8".

Cast iron cutter for Havana Cigars of Excellent Quality. Brunhoff base no. 216, 6.5" x 9".

Cast iron cutter for Betsy Ross, A.S. Valentine & Son, Makers, Philadelphia. Brunhoff base No. 216, Pat. Appl'd For on handle, 6.5" x 8".

Smoke 10 Cent Cigar marquee with Spana Leo insert, Cast iron, Brunhoff base no. 216, 6.5" x 9".

Cast iron cutter for La Dolorita, High Grade Cigar. Brunhoff base No 216, patented Oct. 7, 1902. 6.5" x 9".

Cast iron El Verso cigar cutter, The Diesel Wemmer Co. Brunhoff base 240. Patented Oct. 7, 1902. 7" x 7".

Cast iron cutter advertising Havana Rope, Havana Cigars of Excellent Quality. Brunhoff base 202, 9" x 7".

Cast iron cutter, Irish Lad cigars "Will Dance Into Your Favor", W.A. Davis, Syracuse, N.Y. Brunhoff base 202, 9" x 7".

Leda Cigar cutter. 9" x 7.5", Brunhoff, No 202B.

Right: Cast iron cutter advertising the Welcome Arch, The Struby-Estabrook Mercantile Co., Denver. Patented Oct, 7, 1902, Brunhoff base 202, 9" x 7".

Below: Smokecraft Segars cutter. Patented Oct. 7, 1902, Brunhoff model 250, 4.75" x 7".

Above: 124 The Right Number cigars, W.A. Davis. Syracuse, N.Y. Cast iron, Brunhoff, 8.5" x 6.5".

John. C. Herman and Co.'s King Oscar Cigar cutter with press down lever. Brunhoff. 9" x 7".

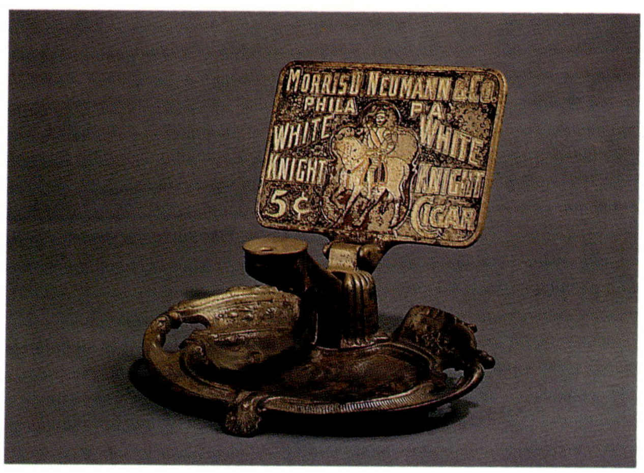

Cast iron cutter advertising White Knight Cigars, Morris D. Neumann & Co., Philadelphia, Pennsylvania. Brunhoff base 202, 9" x 7".

Right: A view of the back of the Trojan Girl cutter.

Below Right: El Santo Cigars cutter, Wise El Santo Cigar Co. Makers, St. Louis. Glass base, iron top. 6.5" x 4.5".

Below: Bachelor Cigars, Andrew Wilson & Company. Two hole cutter, Brunhoff Advertising Specialties, 9" x 9", cast iron.

Above: A double lever cutter advertising Declarencia Havana Cigars. Brunhoff. 8" x 5".

Right: Seal of Minnesota Cigars. Two hole model by Brunhoff, 8.5" x 9".

Two hole cutter advertising Que Placer Havanas. Copyright Louis Y. Aronson, 1918. 5" x 8", brass.

Two double cutter Que Placer Cigar advertising pieces. Copyright Louis Y. Aronson, 1918, 5" x 8".

Roi Tan Cigar two lever cigar cutter with a wonderful advertising piece. The car is tin with a two sided sign that advertising Roi-Tan's campaign of giving away a 1939 Chevrolet each day. The other side invites you to "Take a Ride with Sophie," advertising Sophie Tucker and her Roi-Tan Show on the C.B.S. radio.

Large shell-type cigar cutter, from an actual artillery shell. F.H.S. 195 on side, five size holes, U.M.C. Co., Bridgeport, Conn., U.S.A. on bottom. 2" x 10".

Right: Probably a favorite at the cigar store or the local pub, this is a combination strength-tester and cigar cutter called the Handgrip Test. The cigar cutting is easy; just push down the spring loaded cutter at the top of the column. The strength test is tougher, measuring the power of the grip. This is a great advertising piece for the Grip Cigar, Farrington Cigar Company, New York. The scales read G.B. Fowler Inv. Patd June 22, 1895. Bottom has label still intact, describing The Handgrip Test, 7" x 13".

Below: Pair of cigar cutter "Odd or Even" games, with very similar shape and bases. Left: Pilot Cigar Cutter; right: Smokettes Cigars, Owell, Smith & Co., New York, with polychrome wheel in four colors. 6" x 7.5".

Above: These two cutters and match dispensers are the same model but with different logos. By pushing the finger pads the cigar is cut and a match retrieved from the reservoir below. Left: Barrister Cigar, Celestino Costelo & Co.; right: Bachelor Cigar, Victor Thorsch Co. Makers. 4.75" x 8", cast iron. "Pat Appld for J.M. Co. Mil, Wis" on bottom of both.

Left: This delightful fellow has a cigar cutter in his throat, triggered by pushing down on the head. Painted tin, it has Drücke-Berger painted on chest and RUPPY on bottom. 5" x 5".

Usher's Whiskey mirror with matchsafe and cigar cutter.

Reid & Co's Success, Milton, Pa. 20th Century, Philadelphia, Pennsylvania, 3.5" x 5.5".

Metal cigar cutter in a horseshoe shape advertising Walter R. Gould & Co.'s Newport Cigars. 6" x 7".

This iron cutter advertises Wertheim and Schiffer's World Cigar Cutters. The globe in the middle has the slogan: "Our Field." Dated April 21, 1887. 4" x 4.75".

Peter Pan cutter and a kerosene lighter with pierced lamp shade and two dips. Brunhoff base 931. 9" x 20". Beside it is a cast iron Peter Pan Cigar tip tray. Brunhoff Advertising Specialties, no. 2.

The reverse painted plaque of this cutter and kerosene lighter advertises Cressman's Counsellor Cigars. Brunhoff Manufacturing Company, Cincinnati, Ohio. 7.5" x 15".

Lillian Russell cast iron countertop lighter and cutter with two dips. Brunhoff Mfg. Co., Cinn., Ohio, base 261. 7.5" x 18" x 11".

Paul Jones Havana Cigars countertop lighter, automatic cutter, and lamp with two dips. Brunhoff No. 202 base, 10" x 13" x 13".

Cutter and kerosene lighter. The marquee advertises Austrienne 5 cent cigars. The pierced lamp shade is for Lironda cigars. Metal. 6" x 14".

Cast iron cutter advertising College Widow Cigars. The kerosene lighter has a pierced lamp shade, two dips. J.K. Pfatzgraff & Co., Makers, York-PA., Brunhoff base and patent dates Oct. 7 1902. Base 931. 9" x 20".

Dextet Cigar kerosene lighter and cutter with two dips. Cast iron base, 4" x 9" x 8".

Cutter and kerosene lighter advertising Eisenlohr's Girard Cigars. The cutter is lever activated.

F & D Perfectos are advertised on this combination lighter and cutter. Coppertoned white metal with glass globe. 5" x 10".

Austrienne Cigar cutter and kerosene lighter. 7.5" x 14.5".

Iron and wood electric lighter and cutter for Favorite of Frederick Cigars, Rice & Haller, Frederick, Maryland. 7" x 12". Abbot Electric Company.

Cigar cutter and lighter, advertising La Amenidad Cigars, Joseph Klein & Co Mfg., New York, 10" x 7.5".

Flor de Franklin aptly used this electric lighter and cigar cutter to advertise their product. The image of Ben Franklin, the father of electricity, is reverse painted on the glass marquee. Brunhoff Mfg. Co., metal with wooden base, 10.5" x 8".

Metal Piedmont cigar cutter with a kerosene lamp and pierced lamp shade, and a holder for cigarettes and matches. "The Cigarette of Quality", Piedmont, on glass marquee. Brunhoff Mfg. Co., Cinn., Ohio. 8.25" x 12.25".

Non-Advertising Countertop Cutters / Lighters

Advertising Lighters

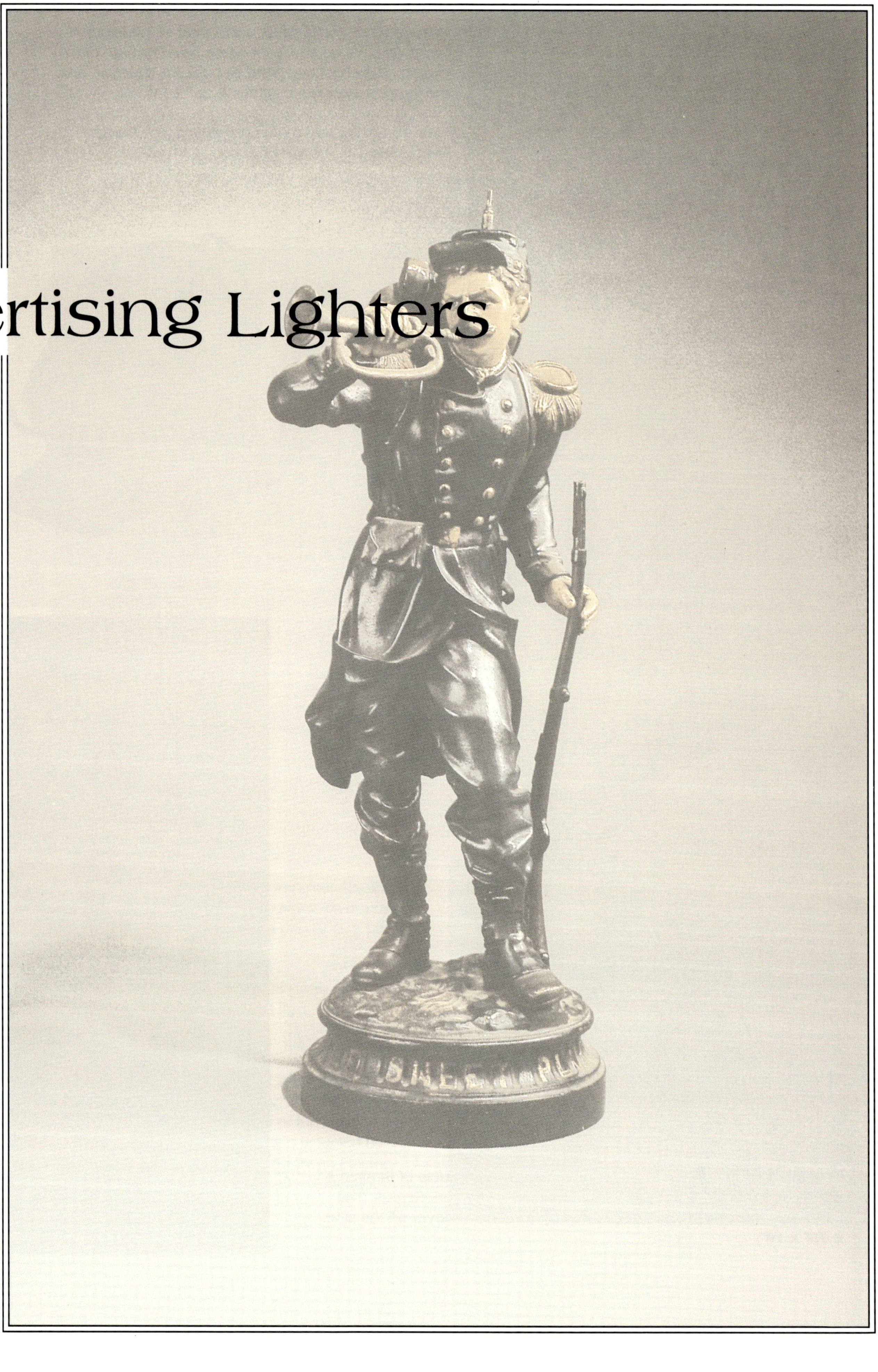

Countertop lighter and lamp, with two dips. The lamp shade is perforated tin and reads Union Made, Dartmouth Club. The base is cast iron and has the same logo as the shade. Kerosene, 6.75"" x 11".

Three Lillian Russell Cigar countertop lighters. Kerosene with two dips. They have perforated tin lamp shades reading "Lillian Russell 5 Cent Cigar," and a marquee on the cast iron base that reads the same. Brunhoff Mfg. Co., 6.75" x 11".

Cressman's Counsellor cigar lighter with marquee, glass kerosene reservoir and pierced tin shade. 7" x 12".

Cressman's Counsellor Cigar lighter. Metal with green glass globe. Brunhoff Manufacturing Company, base number 258L. 7.5" x 13".

Kerosene lighter for Cressman's Counsellor cigars with a blue glass reservoir and pierced shade. 6" x 12".

Left: The marquee of this countertop kerosene lighter advertises Grand Order Cigar. It has a glass globe and two dips. 9.25" x 14".

Right: This metal-based kerosene lighter has a glass marquee that can be used to advertise various cigars, in this case Vincent's 76 Cigar. The lamp has a glass shade and it one dip. Brunhoff Mfg. Co., 9" x 11.5".

Left: Cobalt glass and metal kerosene lighter advertising The Dominator Cigar Factory, H. Muller & Son, New York. 7.5" x 13".

Right: This Wedding Bouquet countertop kerosene lighter has a colored glass globe and a dip on each side of the reservoir to transfer the flame. Wedding Bouquet was made by L. Kahner & Co., New York, 6" x 18".

Left: Kerosene lighter lamp, with glass bulb, painted with Smoke El Vino Cigars. 6" x 15.5".

Right: This kerosene advertising lighter has place for paper advertising in the frame in its base and in its glass globe. This one has a Cinco globe and a Famous 55 Cigar label in the frame. 7.5" x 13.5".

Left: This beautiful glass and cast iron Counsellor lighter features an etched glass shade, a decorated glass reservoir, and nicely cast marquee. Cressman's, Philadelphia. Brunhoff Mfg. Co. 6" x 20".

Right: This elegant countertop lighter has a reverse painted glass reservoir, a marble base, glass globe, and Bakelite dips. It advertises No. 1 Cut & Dry Smoking Tobacco & Copenhagen Snuff. 4" x 14.25".

Left: These swordsmen are gas lighters advertising Kinsmen Cigars. The figures were sculpted by C.H. Masse and the figures are signed. 9" x 24".

Right: A Roman soldier holding a flaming torch for the cigar smoker's convenience. "Smoke Sentinels" is painted on the base of this white metal gas fired countertop lighter. 10" x 18.5".

Left: Roanoke Cigars uses this maiden to advertise their product. Countertop gas lighter, white metal, 10" x 22".

Right: This bugle playing soldier advertises Bugle Sweet Plug tobacco. Countertop gas lighter, white metal, 11" x 20.5".

A magnificent countertop lighter, gas, advertising Aero Cigars with Prometheus atop the aeroplane. 6" x 24", white metal.

Bronzed metal electric/gasoline lighter. The handles flips down to generate a spark which lights the gasoline flame. Two ounces of gas are in the handle, which reads: Our Special, Pat. Mar. 7 93, July 10, 94.

Cast iron lighter advertising El Principe de Gales Havana Cigars, 8" x 11". The hollow brass tip tray advertises the same smoke, 6.5" x 6.5".

Copper striker lighter, featuring Gobbo, the Smiling God of Good Fortune. Thomson & Sproull, Pittsburgh, Pennsylvania. 3" x 5.5".

This is an appropriate advertising lighter for Ram's Horn Cigars. Polychrome white metal, the gas flame comes from the top of the plant. 5" x 8.5".

Left: ceramic humidor with the figure holding a big cigar. Marked 35 inside lid. 5" x 9". Right: an original cast iron humidor. This has been reproduced, and the reproductions have noticeable nut and bolt brackets on the inside. This advertises La Rosa Cigars. 5" x 9".

Metal counter stand and lighter. It holds a box of cigars, which may be lighted with the electric lighter on the front lip of the stand. Brunhoff, Cincinnati, Ohio. 8" x 09/" x 09/.5".

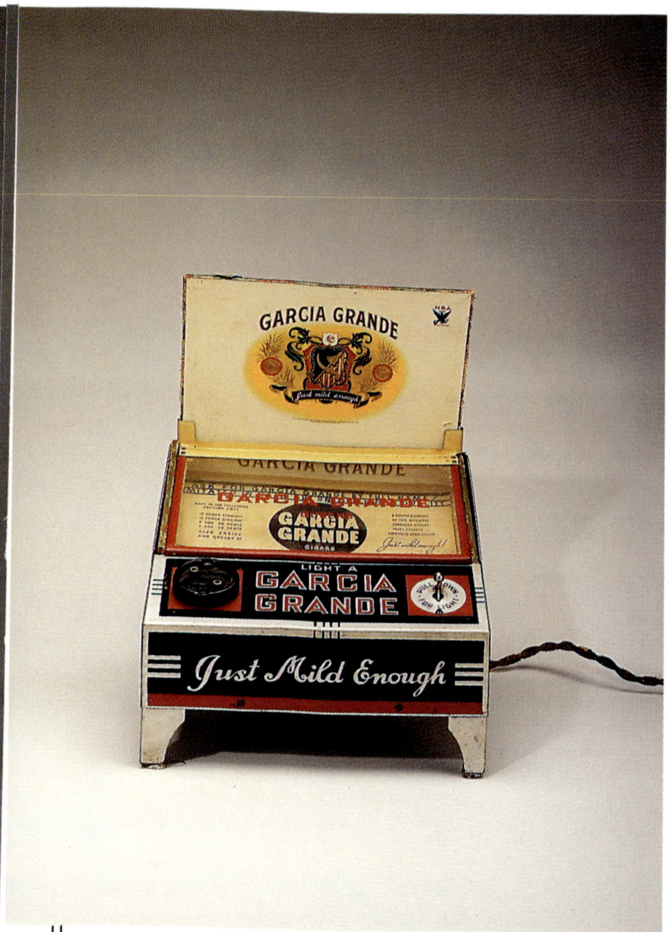

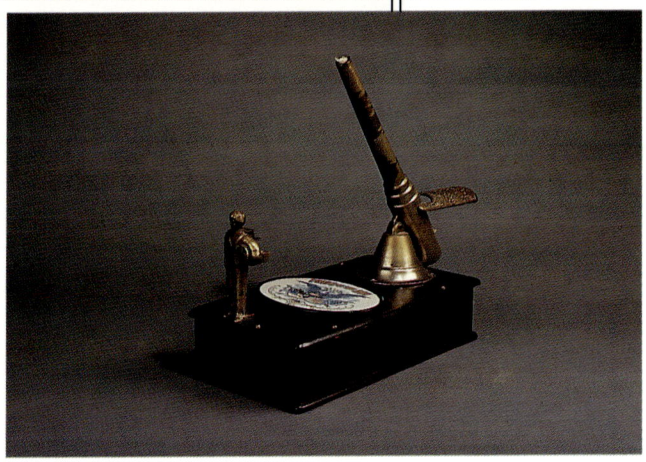

Above and Above: This Chicago Electric Lighter advertises Pride of the Age cigars. The wick in the mouth of the cannon is fueled with gasoline or kerosene, which is lighted by a magneto when the barrel is raised. 14" x 12".

Right: White metal coal oil lighter. The cigar in this figure's mouth was constantly lighted. A match was taken from the basket to transfer the flame to the smoker's cigarette or cigar. 7" tall.

Below: Brass kerosene lighter and matchholder. The reservoir is in the ape's body and the flame comes out from the cigar it is smoking. Signed Fauque. 5" x 6".

Right: Handmade electric lighter, 14" x 25", wood and copper.

Far Right: Wood and brass, the lighter is ignited by pulling it forward. The Wireless, Eldred Mfg. Co., No. 12, Chicago, Pat Applied for. 7.5" x 15.5".

Right: The Wireless in the extended, lit position.

Far Right: Brass and copper coal oil lighter. The wick is under the hinged top brass piece. The handle allows it to either sit on a countertop or hang from the wall. 6.5" tall.

Bibliography

Alsford, Denis B. *Matchholders: 100 Years of Ingenuity.* Atglen, Pennsylvania: Schiffer Publishing Ltd., 1994.

Baer, Willis N., Ph.D. *The Economic Development of the Cigar Industry in the United States*. Lancaster, Pennsylvania: The Art Printing Co., 1933.

Brongers, Georg A. *Nicotiana Tabacum: The History of Tobacco and Tobacco Smoking in the Netherlands*. Groningen, Holland: Theodorus Niemeyer, 1964.

Cigar Institute of America, The. *The Story of Cigars*. New York, 1942.

Congdon-Martin, Douglas. *Tobacco Tins: A Collector's Guide.* Atglen, Pennsylvania: Schiffer Publishing, Ltd., 1992.

__________. America For Sale: A Collector's Guide to Antique Advertising. Atglen, Pennsylvania: Schiffer Publishing, Ltd., 1991.

Cooper, Patricia Ann. *From Hand Craft to Mass Production: Men, Women, and Work Culture in American Cigar Factories, 1900-1919, Doctoral Thesis.* Ann Arbor: University Microfilms International, 1981.

Davidoff, Zino. *The Connoisseur's Book of the Cigar*. New York: McGraw-Hill, 1967.

Davidson, Joe. *The Art of the Cigar Label.* Secaucus, New Jersey: Wellfleet Press, 1989.

Edward Miller & Company Illustrated Catalogue of Bronzed, Decorated, and Real Bronze Lamps and Cigar Lighters. Meriden, Conn., U.S.A. Store No. 35, Warren Street, Corner Church, New York, 1881. Reproduced in 1976 by Fairweather Antiques, Meriden, CT 06450.

Infante, G. Cabrera. *Holy Smoke.* New York: Harper & Row, 1985.

Petrone, Gerard S. M.D. *The Seduction of America: 100 Years of Tobacco Advertising (1830-1930).* Atglen, Pennsylvania: Schiffer Publishing Ltd., 1996.

R.J. Reynolds. *Golden Leaves.* Winston-Salem: 1986.

Price Guide

The price ranges below reflect the best information that could be obtained by the authors from their own experience and the experience of others. They represent an estimate of the value of the item if found on the market in fine condition. They may vary from region to region, dealer to dealer, and even day to day. Use them only as a guide to relative value. The authors and publishers can assume no responsibility for any losses or gains the reader may experience by using this guide. All figures are in U.S. currency.

Page	Position	Value
15	L	1500-2000
	TR	1500-2000
	BR	700-900
16	TL	2000-2500
	BL	1500-2000
	R	2000-2400
17	TL	1200-2000
	BL	1500-2000
	R	1500-2000
18	TL	900-1200
	BL	1000-1300
	TR	1200-1500
	BR	1700-2200
19	TL	500-650
	BL	500-650
	TR	900-1200
	BR	1000-1200
20	T	1000-1200
	C	850-1200
	B	500-800
21	TL	300-550
	CL	900-1200
	BL	350-500
	TR	1200-1500
22	TL	750-1000
	BL	450-650
	TR	600-850
	BR	500-700
23	T	660-850
	C&B	5000-7000
24	L	2500-3000
	T&CR	3500-4000
	B	3500-4000
25		4500-5000
26	L	4500-5000
	TR	1700-2200
	CR	1000-1500
	BR	1500-2000
27	TL	600-900
28	T	2500-3000
	C	1000-1300
	B	350-500
29	TL	500-750
	BL	550-800
	TR	700-900
	BR	600-1000
30	T	600-900
	C	500-700
	B	500-700
31	T	500-700
	C	500-750
	B	500-700
	R	600-850
32	L	500-650
	TR	400-650
	BR	450-600
33	T	250-450
	C	250-350
	B	1500-2000
34	TL	1500-2000
	TR	600-900
	B	600-850
35	L	550-800
	R	1000-1200
	BR	250-550
36	T	1000-1500
	C	1500-1800
	B	1000-1500
37	T	300-500
	B	2200-2800
38	TL	1000-1300
	BL	1500-2000
	TR	600-900
	BR	600-1500
39	T	600-900
	C	2500-3000
	B	950-1500
40	TL	700-950
	BL	350-500
	TR	600-900
	BR	300-400
41	TL	350-500
	B	300-550
	TR	300-500
42	TL	300-550
	BL	450-650
	TR	300-550
	BR	350-450
43	TL	600-900
	TC	600-900
	BL	600-950
	TR	450-650
	BR	500-900
44	L	300-550
	TR	600-900
	BR	600-800
	CR	300-450
45	TL	300-450
	CL	1700-2200
	BL	1200-1500
	R	3000-4000
46	TL	300-450
	BL	350-450
	TR	350-500
	BR	900-1200
47	T	250-400
	C	500-750
	B	500-750
48	TR	600-800
	1CR	500-650
	2CR	500-650
	BR	600-900
49		600-900
50	TL	400-550
	BL	600-900
	TR	600-750
	BR	400-600
51	TL	175-300
	BL	300-500
	TR	800-1000
	BR	400-600
52	T	300-450
	B	800-1200
53	T	3000-4000
	C	500-750
	B	300-500
54	L	500-600
	TR	900-1200
	BR	1200-1500
	CR	1700-2200
55	TL	600-900
	CL	300-550
	BL	200-350
	R	600-900
56	T	250-450
	C	250-350
	B	200-350
57	T&BL	3000-4000
58	TR	250-400
	BR	600-950
	BL	600-700
	TL	850-1000
59	TL	450-700
	BL	450-700
	T&BC	450-700
	R	450-700
60	TL	600-900
	BL	400-600
	TR	350-500
	BR	450-700
61	TL	400-600
	BL	400-600
	R	600-900
62	TL	750-1500
	TR	750-2000
	C&BR	350-600
64	TL	300-450
	BL	150-300
	TR	400-600
	BR	200-300
65	TL	150-300
	CL	200-300
	BL	500-700
	R	450-700
66	L	600-900
	TR	200-350
	CR	250-350
	BR	300-450
67	TL	2000-2500
	BL	300-450
	TR	250-350
68	TL	270-350
	BL	400-550
	TR	200-350
	BR	200-350
69	T	200-300
	C	200-300
	B	175-250
70	L	175-250
	TR	200-300
	CR	200-300
	BR	450-600
71	TL	250-400
	CL	250-450
	BL	250-400
72	TL	175-250
	BL	175-250
	TR	500-600
	BR	3500-4500
73	TR	400-600
	BL	5000-6000
	TL	3500-4500
	BR	400-600
74	BL	3500-4000
	TR	350-500
	CR	200-400
	BR	200-500
75	TL	200-400
	BL	250-550
	TR	250-600
	BR	1700-2200
76	TR	400-650
	L	200-250
	CR	300-450
	BR	200-450
77	T	900-1200
	C	350-500
	B	400-500
78	TL	250-500
	BL	250-350
	TR	350-500
	BR	350-450
79	TL	300-550
	BL	150-300
	TR	350-500
	BR	250-350
80	TL	200-300
	BL	350-500
	TR	300-450
	BR	200-300
81	TL	250-400
	BL	150-350
	TR	250-450
	BR	250-350
82	T	250-350
	C	250-450
	B	600-850
83	TL	250-800
	BL	450-750
	TR	450-650
	BR	300-650
84	BR	200-450
	BL	200-600
	TR	300-450
	TL	200-400
85	TL	250-550
	BR	350-500
	BL	175-300
	TR	500-700
	BR	200-700
86	TL	250-600
	BL	250-550
	TR	250-500
	BR	250-500
88	TL	2000-2500
	BL	1500-2000
	TR	3500-4000
	BR	1700-2000
90	TL	150-500
	BL	250-600
	TR	300-800
	BR	175-450
91	TL	200-400
	BL	150-550
	TR	300-700
	BR	300-700
92	TL	175-600
	B	1750-2000
	TR	300-700
94	TL	1200-1500
	TR	350-500
	BL	300-500
	BC	400-500
	BR	1500-2000
95	TL	550-800
	TR	250-350
	BL	350-500
	BC	150-250
	BR	250-350
96	TL	350-600
	TR	500-700
	BL	300-500
	BC	250-400
	BR	650-800
97	TL	350-550
	TC	400-550
	TR	300-600
	BL	350-550

	BC	500-600
	BR	800-950
98	TL	450-600
	TR	250-450
	CL	200-400
	CR	250-450
	BL	2000-2500
	BC	2000-2200
	BR	250-550
99	TL	500-750
	TR	400-550
	CL	250-550
	CC	450-650
	CR	350-550
	BL	250-450
	BR	250-400
100	TL	300-500
	1CL	700-950
	2CL	200-400
	BL	250-450
	TR	200-300
	BR	250-400
101	TL	350-550
	BL	200-400
	TR	250-450
	BR	350-550
102	TL	500-650
	CL	300-400
	BL	300-450
	TR	100-200
	CR	150-300
	BR	150-350
103	TL	400-600
	BL	200-350
	TR&C	300-500
	BR	400-550
104	TL	200-400
	BL	200-350
	TR	300-500
	CR	250-400
	BR	150-350
105	TL	1500-2000
	BL	200-350
	TR	200-350
	BR	900-1200
109	TL	700-1000
	TR	2200-2600
	BL	500-800
	BC	500-800
	BR	600-900
110	TL	500-800
	TR	600-900
	BL	600-900
	BC	500-800
	BR	500-800
111	TL	600-900
	TR	600-900
	BL	600-900
	BC	500-800
	BR	500-800
112	TL	550-850
	CL	550-850
	BL	600-900
	TR	600-900
	CR	500-800
	BR	600-900
113	TL	550-800
	CL	600-900
	BL	600-900
	TR	600-900
	CR	600-800
	BR	550-800
114	TL	1200-1500
	CL	550-750
	BL	550-800
	TR	350-550
	CR	500-900
	BR	900-1100
115	T&BL	3500-5000
	TC	1200-1500
	CC	650-950
	BC	1500-2000
	R	3500-5000
116	TL	800-1100
	CL	2500-3000
	BL	1500-2000
	TR	800-1100
	CR	1500-1700;
		800-1000
	BR	750-950
117	TL	1500-2000
	CL	800-1100
	BL	800-1100
	R	800-1100
118	TR	1000-1500
	BR	1000-1500
120	TL	500-700
	BL	750-1000
	TR	750-1000
	CR	750-1000
	BR	750-1000
121	TL	750-1000
	1CL	750-1000
	2CL	500-700
	BL	750-1000
	TR	750-1000
	CR	750-1000
	BR	750-1000
123	TR	800-1100
	BL	1500-2000
	TC	2000-2500
	BC	2000-2500
	TL	800-1100
	BR	1500-2000
124	TL	550-800
	CL	1500-2000
	BL	400-700
	TR	1500-2000
	BR	400-700
	C	400-700
125	TL	500-700
	BL	500-800
	TR	500-700
	BR	500-700
126	TL	400-800
	BL	150-200
	TR	500-700
	BC	500-700
	BR	500-700
128	TL	200-350
	BL	500-700
	TR	500-700
	BR	500-700
129	TL	500-700
	BL	500-800
	TR	500-700
	BC	500-800
	BR	500-700
130	TL	500-700
	BL	500-700
	TR	550-800
	BR	500-700
131	TL	500-700
	CL	500-700
	BL	500-700
	TR	500-700
	BR	500-700
132	L	400-700
	TR	900-1200;
		400-700
	CR	400-700
	BR	400-700
133	L	1500-2000
	TC	1500-2000
	TR	1500-2000
	CR	1500-2000
	BL	1500-2000
	BR	1500-2000
134	TL	2200-2500
	BL	2200-2500
	TR	750-950
	BR	2200-2500
135	TL	1200-1500
	TR	900-1200
	B	1500-2000
137	TL	750-1000
	CL	500-700
	BL	500-700
	TR	600-750
	BR	750-1000
138	TL	700-900
	BL	700-900
	CR	350-550
	BR	700-900
139	TL	350-500
	BL	350-500;
		400-600
		(car)
	TR	300-450
	BR	250-400
140	TL	300-500
	BL	200-300
	TR	250-400
	CR	250-400
	BR	250-350
141	TL	1500-2200
	CL	500-700
	BL	2200-3000
	TR	1500-2200
	BR	1500-2200
142	TL	250-500
	CL	250-500
	BL	250-500
	TR	750-900
	BR	750-900
143	TL	350-550
	BL	300-500
	TR	1000-1200
	CR	700-1200
	BR	450-600
144	TL	750-1000
	TR	2000-2500
	BL	450-600
	BC	1700-2200
	BR	2500-3000
145	TL	1200-1500
	BL	1200-1500
	TR	2500-3000
	BR	2000-3000
146	TL	1200-1500
	BL	750-1000
	TR	3000-3500
	BR	700-900
147	TL	3000-4500
	BL	350-500
	TR	400-500
	BR	350-500
149	TL	1500-2000
	BL	1500-2000
	TC	1200-1600
	BC	1200-1600
	R	1500-2000
150	L	1800-2200
	TC	2000-2500
	BC	1500-2200
	TR	3000-4500
	BR	2500-3000
151	TL	4000-5000
	BL	2500-3500
	TC	1500-2000
	BC	1500-2000
	R	2500-3000
152	TL	750-1200
	BL	3000-4000
	TR	3000-3800
	CR	3000-4000
	BR	1500-2000
153	TL	2500-3500
	TR	900-1200
	BR	900-1200
	BL	1000-1200
154	TL	2000-3000
	BL	1500-2200
	TR	2000-3000
	BR	2000-3000
156	L	2500-3000
	C	750-2000
	TR	1000-2000
	BR	550-750
157	TL	1500-2000
	BL	150-250
	TR	450-600
	BR	3000-4500
159	TL	1500-2000
	TR	1500-2500
	BL	1700-2000
	BC	1700-2000
	BR	1700-2000
160	TL	3500-4500
	BL	1200-1500
	TR	1200-1500
	BR	5000-7000
161	TL	700-900
	BL	5000+
	TR	3000-4500
	BR	4000-6000
162	TL	8000+ pr.
	BL	5000+
	TR	5000+
	BR	7000+
163		6000-8000
164	TL	1500-2500
	TR	5000+
	BL	1200-1500
	BC	250-300
165	TL	200-400
	TR	800-1200
	BL&R	4000-6000
167	TL	1500-3000
	BL	1500-2000
	TR	3000-5000
	BR	900-1200
168	TL	750-1200
	BL	2500-3500
	TR	600-1000
	BR	2000-3000
169	TL	750-1000
	BL	750-1000
	TR	750-1000
	BR	500-750
170	L	500-750
	TC	4000-5500
	BC	4000-5000
	TR	3000-4500
	BR	2500-4000
171	BL	2500-3500
	TC	2000-3000
	TL	300-500
	BC	3000-5000
	R	3500-5000
172	TL	5000+
	TC	3500-5000
	TR	1200-1500
	BC	2500-4000
	BR	3500-5000
	BL	1500-1700
173	TL	3500-5000
	TC	700-900
	TR	1200-1500
	BL	5000+
	BC	900-1200
	BR	4500-6000
174	T	500-750
	L	1200-1500
	CC	1000-1500
	CR	1000-1200
	BR	450-550